Praise for *Cultivating Redemption*

"Wow! Crystal has shined her light with grace and hope into the deep darkness of abuse, trauma, and pain. Her experience may be different from yours, but all of us know the deep brokenness of our human condition. She helps us understand our pain and our deceptions by shining gospel grace that brings hope and healing, not shame and condemnation. May her courage and her story, empowered by Scripture, bring hope and healing to thousands."

—**Dr. Leo Endel**, executive director, Minnesota-Wisconsin Baptist Convention; author, *Life is All About Relationships*

"Author, Crystal Persons, invites readers to walk with her as she shares her uniquely introspective and interactive personal narrative. Crystal recounts the initial traumas of her youth, her moments of making room for brokenness, and her struggle to pursue authentic healing. She provides the reader with biblical truths and bolstering resources which have encouraged her along her journey.

Cultivating Redemption enables the reader to identify possible personal and private enslavement to past traumas, and provides proven insights as to how readers may realize, understand, and experience true, biblical redemption–not just the moment of salvation, but the joint-journey with Jesus. While honestly confronting the damage done in the past, Crystal illustrates how Jesus leads the reader through their brokenness in order to transform and sanctify the physical, mental, emotional, and spiritual lives of Christ-followers.

Readers will appreciate how moments of holy discontentment prompted Crystal to pursue a deeper understanding of her own redemption as it also continues to clearly direct her steps toward her own personal ministry. Even in the midst of present suffering, or when we are reflecting on the scars of past suffering, Cultivating Redemption reminds us that we were bought for a price and bought for a purpose; a purpose he pre-ordained uniquely…for you."

—**Michael D. Rumsey**, small group leader; educator; writer

"Cultivating Redemption is a soul-searching handbook for any believer who desires the freedom that comes from walking fully surrendered with Jesus. Crystal vulnerably walks us through the very things that enslaved her for years, and invites us to journey with her to know God as both tender and present. This book will open your eyes to the ways you have been holding back the less-desirable parts of your story and compel you to allow Jesus to start putting them to work for you instead of against you!"

— **Niccie Kliegl** CEO, Fulfill Your Legacy; business coach; author, *The Legacy Series*

CULTIVATING REDEMPTION

finding freedom through the darkness

CRYSTAL PERSONS

Printed in the United States of America

2024 First Edition
Ebook ISBN - 978-1-965905-02-9
Paperback ISBN - 978-1-965905-03-6
Hardcover ISBN - 978-1-965905-04-3

Published by Bright Ink Press
12 Boulevard, Tallapoosa, GA 30176

DEDICATION

To my husband, Chris: You have never silenced me but freed me to find my voice in my healing journey. When God calls me to do hard things, you humbly encourage me to take those steps of obedience, without hesitation. Your unwavering support—of me writing this book and becoming who He created me to be—has been nothing short of God's intimate, sacrificial love poured out. There is no one I would rather do life and Kingdom work alongside!

To my children–Krispen, Krysiana, and Krystazya: You are the reason I had to be brave enough to face my past trauma. Your innocent, trusting nature—inviting me into your daily fears and struggles—keeps me running back to Jesus' presence. I pray the way I love you lays a redemptive foundation for Him to build your stories upon. May you always trust Him fully and know deeply where your inherent worth is found.

CONTENTS

PART 1

DEVELOP AWARENESS

CHAPTER 1

WHAT IS IT

I do not take for granted that you are here, sharing this space with me. My deepest desire is that you would discover within these pages both the positional and functional application of redemption, as I am actively discovering the latter for myself. We all have brokenness as part of our stories. One in five people have trauma in their past[1] with up to 20% of those traumatized developing Post Traumatic Stress Disorder (PTSD). For those who have experienced severe trauma, 60-80% develop PTSD.[2] Severe traumatization is often the effect of war, sexual abuse, and near-death experiences. PTSD is not a switch that can be turned off and on, nor does it mean that the individual who suffers is unwilling to apply Biblical truths to their brokenness. It is crucial we understand how trauma affects the brain from a neuroscience perspective, but only to help build a foundation of understanding in this first chapter as it is not my field of expertise. Most importantly, I want to infuse hope for healing because where there is brokenness, there is space for redemption.

I will be weaving my own story of trauma and PTSD throughout this book. Mine is from sexual trauma. Even as I just wrote these words, I paused to reach out to a friend who was the first to name my trauma during our freshman year of high school…"Crystal, that's rape."

I just now thanked her again for inserting some clarity into my extremely disoriented state. I remember the inability to absorb this truth at the time, while simultaneously feeling that it was indeed truth. I immediately filed it away, inwardly vowing to never share my story again because the burden of it was far too great for me to bear on my own. It would be years before I would share it again, and not until God Himself moved me to do so. When I did share, it felt radical–going against every human impulse within me. In fact, it wasn't me at all, but the Spirit working within me to usher in healing and much-needed grace for the journey ahead. So much more on this later.

Do you have a secret deep within you that's desperate to get out?

Another person comes to mind as I write. He wasn't one of my abusers, but an informant of sorts. My abusers would get information from him. He was my age, just a kid himself. I can remember his face, eyes wide with fear, the few times he came to pick me up and take me to a predetermined location. And then he was gone. I wonder if reaching out to him and telling him I'm okay–that life is beautiful for me now–might help him heal from his past trauma too. Is he even in a healthy enough spot to receive this message from me? Is he safe for me to invite back into my life in this way? I don't have answers to these questions. Still, there is purpose in asking them.

Where is this sympathy coming from toward someone who played a part in my abuse?

I share all this so you can witness how Jesus is leading me to struggle forward in my healing. When things come to mind regarding my past, I'm learning to invite Jesus into those inner conversations instead of stuffing them back down into the abyss of my unhealed self. I've learned to trust that if a memory surfaces, it's because He has allowed it to for a reason. I must ask Him what He wants me to do with it. To be sure, healing and redemption are His purpose. So I lean in to know the next step to take. And I invite you to journey with me, whether in pursuit of your own healing or so you can advocate for the healing of others. Jesus never fails to lead us through our fears and into more freedom than we could possibly know on our own.

Because we all have a level of understanding when it comes to trauma, I have prayed over and sought out definitions that I feel are not only accurate but usher you through the door of divine healing. We cannot experience healing on our own. We were created to be dependent on our Creator. And He is only ever gentle and loving in His pursuit of us.

Trauma defined is emotional distress caused by the recurrent tormenting memory of a horrific event, either witnessed or experienced. We can identify forms of traumatic memories in the lives of war veterans and victims of sexual abuse, domestic violence, or serious accidents. It can be associated with emotional or psychological abuse, threats to life or safety, and significant forms of intimate betrayal. Trauma destroys a world–it upends an entire way of living. Because of this, victims are often overwhelmed by the uprooting of life's meaning and are left desperately searching for new significance.[3]

Redemption is when Jesus buys us back from the slave block. Positionally, God redeems us once and for all the moment we recognize we are sinners in need of a Savior and accept His perfect sacrifice as payment for our sins. There is no undoing this transaction. God declares us righteous and frees us from the bondage and penalty of sin. I learned this fact comprehensively in Bible college. I have never questioned the validity of this truth. But as I entered into the role of pastor's wife, I somehow missed the functional application of this in my own life–particularly regarding those past events that still held my heart and mind in a place of slavery.

"For freedom you have been set free; stand firm, therefore, and do not submit again to a yoke of slavery." –Galatians 5:1

It took me years to recognize I was enslaved to my past trauma. Ten years into marriage and ministry, I knew Jesus was calling me to freedom. My husband,

Chris, used Galatians 5:1 to love me back to Jesus' heart after I attempted to rummage through the details of my past, hoping to heal. But without my permission, my mind and emotions spiraled.

A week went by and I could hardly function. It was as if I had awakened a darkness I couldn't escape. Nightmares became constant, a portal into my worst fears during sleeping hours. There was no rest. And recurring flashbacks of the trauma during my waking hours made it feel like I was living the abuse all over again. What made it worse was that I was now a mom of two littles, and the enemy upped the ante by throwing them into the mix. Life-like nightmares tormented me day and night. I dreamed abusers were trying to break into our home to harm my children the way they had harmed me. Home. Our safe space. It was taken from me in an instant. There was no safe space. And no one understood. How could they? I didn't have words for what was happening inside of me. I felt utterly alone and without hope.

Post Traumatic Stress Disorder (PTSD), according to Christian counselor H. Norman Wright, "is not just an emotional response to troubling events; it's the expression of a persistent deregulation of body and brain chemistry. Brain chemistry can be altered for decades. With this change, arousing events can trigger flashbacks. Trauma creates chaos in our brain. Trauma causes an emotional as well as a cognitive concussion."[4]

Although I felt utterly alone and without hope, Jesus saw me. And He drew near through my husband who was watching all this unfold in real time. Chris could have isolated me in my battle with my trauma, causing me to feel rejected by urging me to pull myself together and then condemning me for my unbelief in who God is and what He can do. But God made sure this wasn't the case. He knew exactly what I needed–truth that would offer real freedom from my torment and a living hope that would be my constant anchor in the storm.

One day, while I was in the midst of this deep struggle, Chris came to me. Filled with the Spirit, he tenderly said, "I have been observing you this week. You are not being led by the Spirit of God but by a spirit of fear. God redeemed you. You are free. But as Galatians 5:1 says, you are still sitting next to the slave block that once held you captive. But you are free. It's time to get up and walk in that freedom. You need to let Jesus functionally redeem your story, Crystal."

He said it most tenderly, yet his words were unwavering. Jesus was calling me back to His presence through my husband. I never decided to leave. But much later, I would learn that my actual brain needed healing too, and that without it, I would continue in seasons of spiraling out of control because of my PTSD.

Here's where the amygdala, the hippocampus, and

the ventromedial prefrontal cortex come into play. (*I promise, you want to know about this...hang in there with me. It matters.*)

Karl Benzio, the Medical Director of the American Association of Christian Counselors, explains it well:

"The emotional center—a structure in our limbic system called the ***amygdala***—becomes overactive when injured. So then our emotions, which God uses as a warning system, become more sensitive. Our brain is on the lookout because we don't want to get hurt again. It searches for situations that are similar to past hurts so we can avoid them. Our emotions are on high alert.

Our memory center—another structure in the limbic system called the ***hippocampus***—shrinks and becomes less active when we are emotionally injured. When a distressing situation occurs, we want to know whether a present danger exists or whether the present situation only slightly resembles a past danger. Our injured hippocampus sometimes can't distinguish past memories, with their attached emotions, from present perceptions.

Our emotional thermostat—known as the ***ventromedial prefrontal cortex*** (VM-PFC)—is underactive when injured. The VM-PFC connects into our limbic system (emotional center) and regulates the intensity of the emotional responses triggered by the amygdala, especially negative emotions such as fear, as well as the reaction we have to the triggering event. The emotional warning signs we experience can be exaggerated because this emotional regulator is inhibited. This is one of the reasons why anxious people or those with PTSD startle easily. Also, the exaggerated reaction doesn't allow the prefrontal cortex "first responder" to perform a reasonable assessment of the present situation and enact a levelheaded response. Instead, our trauma-damaged minds produce impulsive, knee-jerk, survival-oriented, emotionally-driven, dysfunctional decisions."[5]

Okay, take a deep breath. There were a lot of big words in there, but I'm praying it's laying a strong foundation for why we respond how we do to trauma.

Now let's take a moment and talk about prevalence, because authentic healing needs a major bump up on the priority list in our culture if we are to walk in the fullness of who we were created to be. Trauma affects one in five people, including people in the church. But it's rarely obvious who they are. People who have been through trauma react in different ways, making their symptoms difficult to distinguish. Some try to bury the feelings, others are vexed by nightmares, and still others have no idea their past traumas are behind the anxiety or depression they're currently feeling.[1]

It's also helpful to understand that millennials are much more likely than Boomers to report trauma, while Gen X falls between. The most common symptoms include sleep disturbances (52%), ruminating on the traumatic event (49%), and anxiety (49%) among practicing Christians who have been traumatized.[6] This is ample evidence (in case you needed it) that we, as the church, need to make space for healing of past trauma.

Oftentimes, Christians who have experienced trauma either find their comfort in the Bible or struggle to engage with it. If you find yourself in the former camp, keep leaning in. He will complete the work He began in you. But would you also take a moment now and pray about how you can make space for someone else in need of healing? Jesus always desires to multiply His work in us. Steward this beautiful gift of healing. Do it for His glory.

If you are, however, someone who falls into the latter camp, I humbly invite you to engage with God through prayer and His Word anew. I invite you to it because Jesus is freeing me, a pastor's wife, from the sense that I need to appear put together. He is instead giving me the courage to surrender all the parts of my story for His glory and my good. *Even the darkest, scariest parts*. And I know with everything in me that He waits patiently with healing and redemption for you, too.

It is from a place of surrender that I write, asking Him to show up and do what only He can do. My prayer is that you would tangibly feel the pockets of grace He is creating for you as you read, and that you would lean into them with everything you are. Because He did not create you to go it alone. We were designed to walk it out with Him and with others. *You are not alone. There is hope.*

A note for those of you with past trauma, and especially those with PTSD…*I see you.* I know what it feels like to be triggered when engaging with someone else's trauma. I have done my best to write each word from a place of hope. But please keep in mind *this is not a sprint.* Pay attention to how the Spirit is leading you. If you need to step away and grab a cup of coffee, spend some time in His Word and prayer, connect with a trusted friend or counselor, get a good night's sleep, come back next week and pick up where you left off–or if you just need to put the book down entirely because you don't feel that Jesus is asking you to walk through this right now–then DO IT.

He leads us with peace and grace each step of the way. Don't force something outside of His timing for you. But please, *take the next step* He is leading you to take. Remaining where you are is not His heart or purpose for you. There is so much beauty and restoration ahead, and Jesus alone knows the way.

Although my story is unique to me, I believe with my entire being that Jesus wants to storm the darkness with His glorious light, bringing freedom to those captive. And so what I share from various angles, although specific to my story, offers awareness of the darkness that very much exists in every single one of our communities. But I am trusting Jesus to move us beyond mere awareness–to make us plain uncomfortable, and then to normalize discomfort so that our hearts are broken and we are moved to action in one accord with His Spirit of truth, heralding Him as our only Source of comfort…as it should be.

Jesus spent His days in earthly ministry going to the outcasts, the broken, the humble, the lowly, the misunderstood, the rejected, the diseased and the crippled. But our human tendency is to keep a distance so we aren't inconvenienced and don't get hurt. My hope is that you can feel Him beckoning us beyond the restraints of what we currently know in pursuit of more of Him. In our community, in our churches, in our homes, and in ourselves…we desperately need every bit of who He is to penetrate the darkness as we put on the armor and go to battle.

May it be so, Lord Jesus. Make us courageous.

National Statistics (from Guardian Group)

"Unlike some other statistics you have come across in your life, the following stats have a pulse; they are America's daughters, sisters, nieces, and sometimes America's sons as well.

Sex trafficking is a complex crime that is underreported and under-studied. However, progress is being made in trying to change this. A great first step in gaining an overview of the depth of sex trafficking here in the United States is to understand the statistics that have been discovered through good research. For every number you see, please remember that it is not simply a number but instead represents a person; a person who has a name, who had goals and dreams for their life and needs someone to fight for them.

One of the fastest growing criminal industries in the world is the buying and selling of people.

If you think of this crime and these victims in the same manner a predator does, as a product or commodity, the rapid increase makes sense; a person can be sold for a sex act numerous times while a drug or weapon can only be sold once. The internet has also allowed this crime to scale at an incredible pace.

Child sex trafficking is reported in all 50 states.

This is no longer a crime that lives overseas despite what popular movies portray. This is a domestic problem requiring a national community-wide response. Data shows that 83% of victims identified in sex trafficking cases were in the United States legally. Victims are victims regardless of nationality; no person should ever be sold as a commodity. This stat does prove the widely believed misconception that trafficking only happens to those who have crossed an international border."[7]

CHAPTER 2

HOW DO I SORT THROUGH IT ALL

I didn't even know it was there. I thought perhaps forgetting and moving on with my life was the path to becoming someone worthy of God's favor and the approval of others. But what I worked so hard to bury was being unearthed in every thought, every conversation, every decision. It was the evidence of the damage done, and it was constantly working against me and those I love. Forgetting wasn't a step towards healing, but rather an attempt at self-preservation…and it was my personal, silent slavery.

Wasn't everyone expecting perfection from a pastor's wife? I was only 22 years old, but I had a clear image in my mind post-Bible college, and so I hit the "copy & paste" buttons. I had tried hard to be so many different people in my life–walk the walk, talk the talk, dress the dress. I was certain I had to keep my past concealed, but not just from everyone else…I had to keep it locked away and inaccessible, *even from myself.* If I dared to feel–if I allowed myself to remember–it would be the undoing of this new life I was sure needed me to fit the part. *I needed me to fit the part.*

It felt safe. It felt "acceptable to God". It felt admirable, and closer to who I was created to be than any other part I had previously played. Everything I held most dear was in the balance. I had to get this right and maintain it moving forward at all costs.

"One of the reasons we hate our weakness is because it reveals we rely on our strength."

–Dr. Paul David Tripp

My husband and I went straight from Bible college into youth ministry. It was seven years in before I could see some of my teen girls pulling away from me, not relating to the encouragement and caution I shared when it came to dating and remaining pure until marriage. I grew frustrated when my efforts to win them over to what I knew was right fell flat. My repeated attempts, through the overuse of verses and words I had collected from books I read in my young adulthood, only drew more distance between my heart and theirs.

It was then that the Holy Spirit broke through what I knew and opened my eyes to the deeper issue–*it was me*. It may have sufficed for *me* to hit copy and paste, but these girls craved something real, a more authentic connection than I could offer them in my *put-togetherness*.

Something unexpected happened as I imperfectly leaned in to know God's heart for these girls...He brought into focus a truth that would set my heart on a new, terrifying path. For the first time ever, I was certain I needed to share my story. The very things I was certain would get my husband fired and us kicked out of the church, Jesus was asking me to share with my youth girls. It didn't make a bit of sense. I physically trembled at the thought. I didn't even have words for most of my story. But I could not deny His leading me to share, and somehow His love and strength altogether compelled me to make space and invite them in.

How could they share their struggles to apply the truth of God's Word if they believed I had never struggled to do the same? I was maintaining a lie which was completely and utterly unrelatable. It was not welcoming to anyone who was struggling.

"Brokenness is a better bridge for people than my pretend wholeness ever was."

–Sheila Walsh

We took our Minnesota-based youth group on a long bus ride to Spokane, Washington, to assist a local church and friends from Bible college in hosting VBS for their town. I knew this change in setting was where Jesus was asking me to invite them into my brokenness. Chris never once discouraged me from sharing. If he had any reservations about what it would mean for his job at the church, he never spoke a word of them to me. He was only ever encouraging me forward as best he knew how. In doing so, he made sure the schedule that week allowed me an hour alone with the girls.

The day came quickly, and I was somehow grateful it had come. My stomach was in knots for weeks from the anxiety of planning to share, and I was certain that whatever lay on the other side had to feel better than that. The time came. I ugly cried through the entire thing, wrongly assumed personal responsibility for my abuse, and didn't have correct terms for anything that happened to me, other than the one instance my friend boldly called out for me in 9th grade…*rape*. But there was so much more to the story.

I shared in a most messy and utterly imperfect way. How did I not know *how* to tell my own story? I felt thinner than I ever had before in ministry. Like I could crumble at the slightest word of criticism, which I fully expected would rain down on us as soon as we returned home. The sharing of my utmost weakness and brokenness wasn't something I learned how to do in Bible college. I ended by pleading with the girls to be careful with whom they shared my story as I just didn't know how people might use it against Chris and me.

And then, with a teared-soaked page of notes in my trembling hands, I looked up. There wasn't a dry eye in the room. Dear faces of compassion, grace, and understanding met my blurry eyes. Without even giving thought to my actions, I stood up and went to each girl, holding her shoulders while looking directly into her eyes with a resolve and purpose I had never had before. One by one, I encouraged and urged each girl with unrehearsed words that came in the moment I needed them: "We love you. Jesus loves you. Don't settle for less than His best for you." More tears and warm embraces ensued, along with a tenderness in these relationships that has lasted through the years.

Something unexpected happened when I shared my brokenness with those girls–an uncalculated, grace-filled response from them, and a new stirring inside of me to *make space for brokenness*. I didn't yet know Jesus was using this to move me towards healing. It was clearly His work, not mine. I simply surrendered all I had–trauma, fears, and unknown reactions. It didn't seem a proper offering, but He went ahead and multiplied it anyway.

As a pastor's wife with past trauma and PTSD, I am in a position of both needing deep personal healing and feeling the weight of responsibility to make space for others to heal. But it's a crazy beautiful blessing because, in this place, Jesus keeps me close to His heart as I love His people forward. Being wrapped in the humility of my own need for grace guards me from wasting precious energy on maintaining appearances or from the notion that I must have the perfect response in someone's time of need. I have learned that Jesus in the midst of my brokenness means Jesus in the midst of theirs, too.

"Be still, and know that I am God."
—Psalm 46:10

Many professing Christians are spiritually stuck because their view of God is very narrow, as was mine before sharing with my youth girls. If you are like me and have found yourself locked up mentally and emotionally as you commit to journey forward, stilling yourself before Him is the key to personal mobilization. We must proactively create space in our lives to allow the knowledge of who He is to penetrate our worries and our fears, our shame and our regrets. He is always every bit of who He says He is, but a head knowledge will not suffice when freedom is the goal.

"People don't know when they are suppressing their emotions. Therapy is meant to be a part of church discipleship, leadership, and culture, leading people to freedom. We need to teach people to grieve and deal with loss."

–Pete Scazerro

It was April 2014, exactly ten years ago from the moment I type these words, that Jesus asked me to be open to writing a book and sharing my story publicly someday. I kept it close, sharing with only Chris and two or three close friends. I told God that although I was terrified and certainly unqualified, I would surrender my fears so long as He did the *actual work* of making it happen. The shame and condemnation He was actively setting me free from ensured a humble resolve to keep it about Him. Never again did I want to point people to an unattainable and unrealistic image of myself. But if I was going to continue sharing from a place of brokenness, it would only ever be for one reason–to give glory to the One who was taking my story from the grip of Satan and giving it kingdom purpose through His resurrection power.

Nearly a decade after He asked me to be willing to write, He told me to make space to hear His voice. He then specifically brought to mind my Instagram account. I knew immediately I needed to stop posting on Instagram (something I spent time on daily) until I heard what He wanted to tell me. For that entire week I only checked on and responded to messages on that platform. It was a fast of sorts, one that He led me into after hearing a sermon on idols. I didn't know if He was telling me IG was an idol or if He just wanted the extra space to expose the "good things" that were occupying my attention when it needed to be elsewhere. Either way, I obediently made the space.

My posture was that of being on the edge of my seat, waiting for Him to show up. It was anticipatory. Whatever He was leading me to, I sensed it was bigger than me, and I had a growing inclination with each passing hour that it had to do with the book. I brought it up to Chris, and we decided to maintain a watch and pray stance.

That night when I opened up my IG app there was a message waiting for me from someone I had never met before. She thanked me for my Kingdom work in that space. Her specific encouragement felt like God saying, "You are honoring me with this platform, keep cultivating those things that truly matter here." So I thanked her for her timely message and let her in just a bit as to how I was currently holding this account with open hands at the Lord's prompting. We messaged back and forth a few times, going a bit deeper with each correspondence, and then she asked me if I would share my story on her podcast. This request was so specific and seemed an unexpected complement to how God had been asking me to remain open to His use of my story over the years. I told Chris, and we both sensed God was on the move.

"Have a conversation with her and see where it leads," he said. So I did.

In that conversation just a week later, she asked to know more about how God was leading me. She became excited and shared that she leads a non-profit ministry, but also a business that helps female entrepreneurs write their books and get established as authors, coaches, and speakers. Chris and I could not believe it. *Could it be this easy*?! Was God actually doing the *work* of bringing what He called me to into fruition?

He was, and He is.

Had I not chosen to surrender something "good" (Instagram) to be reminded anew that He is God in my midst, I would have never known how He was moving me along in my healing journey. *See the ripple effect?*

Writing is healing for me. I have been inviting people in vulnerably since 2014, knowing that it's one of the main tools He uses to guard me from "submitting again to a yoke of slavery". Small group, one-on-one's over coffee, inviting people into our home, Instagram…and now, writing a book. *This is not me ya'll.* It's completely and utterly Jesus. I stepped out, obedient step after obedient step, because I first heard His tender voice. This allowed Him to penetrate my worst mistakes and biggest regrets–ones that nearly cost me my actual, physical freedom.

As His people, we have the supernatural benefit of sorting through our brokenness how and when He leads us to. He who is our Creator is also the Author of our stories and Redeemer of all that's broken. *No more sitting next to the slave block that once shackled you, friend.* Let us bravely walk together in newness of life in the very face of wreckage.

I was 14 years old, and just about as unsure of myself as a girl could be. A freshman and newbie to the high school landscape, I found myself constantly searching. For what… I didn't know. My heart was restless and vulnerable. I love people, so I was quick to make friends with individuals from all sectors of my public school–the country folk, the religious, the NJROTC patriots, the jocks, the wanna-be ganstas, the theatrically inclined, the singing crowd, the Spanish clubbers. I found common ground with all, except the mean kids. I felt as if my frail vulnerabilities would be exposed if I even came near them. Looking back, they were searching too. Trying to find their place. But they were too brash with their comments, too quick to judge mere appearances, and always ready for a fight. So, I did my best to stay out of their way.

I had played volleyball when I was in junior high, so I figured it was an easy choice when the list of extracurricular activities was in front of me. Besides, I had friends who would be playing too. I grew up with many of the girls signing up for volleyball that fall, but some were new to me. There were some upperclassmen with something to prove, so I decidedly kept with the girls in my own grade.

Soon into the season, one of my new freshman friends on the team announced she would be having a sleepover at her house, and that all the freshman volleyball girls were invited. I told my mom, who asked all the responsible parent questions…"Will her parents be home? Will there be other girls there? Do I have her home phone number?" (Yes, this was before cell phones, people!) Everything on the surface checked out, and any reservations my Mom may have had were quickly overridden by my insistence that I not be the only one left out.

As I write this, my chest is tightening and my breathing becomes more shallow. I almost just kept pushing through with writing but I feel the nudge to invite you into how it feels to share the hard parts of your story with others. Physical reactions are a normal part of working through trauma. If you feel a shift in your body as you step out and share, know that it is normal. It is part of healing. And if Jesus is leading us to venture into the mess, our sharing is not aimless or in vain. Friend, He actively buys your story back from the grips of the enemy as you share.

Let Him bring your darkness into the light where freedom and rest await you.

A note to all the Mamas out there–I am making space for you right here. My own sweet Mama is much on my heart every time I share this part of my story. I can only imagine how she must feel every time she processes it. I'm sure the regret and what-ifs threaten her peace of mind to this day. I'm praying as I write that whatever brokenness comes–*or has come*–into the lives of your children is used to bring them deeper into their relationship with Jesus, and that you would trust His redemptive power far above your ability to protect them from evil. *Jesus can be trusted with their stories too.*

When my mom dropped me off, the girls were heading back to my new friend's bedroom and finding a spot to set their things down. On the way to the bedroom, I caught a brief glimpse of her mom before she retired for the night to her own bedroom on the other side of the house. She seemed normal. Hard working, tired at the end of a long day. If I remember correctly, she worked in realty.

It seems that we had only stood around in my friend's room for a few minutes before a couple of guys came crawling through her ground-level bedroom window. *Couldn't her mom hear what was going on?* I thought it very strange and unexpected. I was caught off guard by it all. *"This would never happen in my house,"* I thought to myself. Nor would I ever have imagined allowing boys to sneak into my bedroom. My dad would have brought that to an end real quickly. It was only a few moments of my new friend and these two men talking quietly while scanning the room before she locked eyes on me, and theirs quickly followed. One boy I vaguely recognized as someone I thought to be my new friend's boyfriend. He was older than we were...around 17. The other man looked a bit older. He was the one who made his way over to me and asked if I would step into the walk-in closet and talk with him.

I had relatively no understanding of just how broken this world could be, and discerning in the moment if this man was a threat seems impossible to me as I look back.

He told me I was beautiful. They were the first words he spoke to me. I felt special and chosen out of a room full of girls. That meant something to me, and it instantly became the basis of all my decisions moving forward.

I felt chosen. I felt set apart. I felt…*safe*?

How Trafficking Happens

From the Guardian Group's 2021 Report on Sex Trafficking in America: "A predator looks for a vulnerability within a victim that can be exploited. This can occur either in-person or online. A predator that assesses and recruits potential victims in-person will often spend time at locations where youth hang out (i.e. school, malls, coffee shops, parks) looking for vulnerabilities within the young people that are there.

A common vulnerability is low self-esteem. A predator can easily spot these traits by simply watching how a young girl reacts when he calls her beautiful. If she lowers her head or shows signs of insecurity, she is potentially a good target."[1]

PART 2

ESTABLISH A SAFE PLACE

CHAPTER 3

MY SHEEP HEAR ME

I felt Him calling me out, away from my poorly constructed shelter. There was no praise song I could sing, no passage of Scripture I could read, no quiet space I could find that wasn't exposing what I had both consciously and subconsciously chosen not to feel. All the emotions swirled around in my soul, begging to find a landing place–somewhere strong enough to house what I was most certain I could not–and someone to create safe passage through the darkest moments of my life. I knew better than to go it alone… it was as if my heart, soul, mind, and will made a collective decision to *seek*. There was no holding back, even if I wanted to. The most intrusive thoughts and physical trauma responses couldn't keep me from leaning in with every broken part of me.

Only One was able to house what I could not and lead me safely on such a treacherous path. An unexpected, gentle voice beckoned me forward. It was a most unfamiliar tone, yet I knew the voice deeply. For the first time in my adult life, I approached the throne of grace with a confidence and assurance that could only be described as *supernatural intervention*.

"My sheep hear my voice, and I know them, and they follow me." –John 10:27

As a child of God, there are many voices contending for, and even demanding, our allegiance and devotion. It is vital that we discern His voice from the voice of the masses. He intimately calls out to us, and if we recognize His voice, we can follow Him into the unknown with everything we are. *If* we recognize His voice.

I am reminded over and over again, through all the pressures in life, that I get to first and foremost be His child. No other title I bear holds power on its own. Wife, mom, daughter, sister, friend–all significant and meaningful–but not one of these roles ascribes my worth or sets me free. When I make space to be near Him, every other relationship I have benefits profoundly.

Being His child means I don't have to know or do all the things. It means that *I get to surrender* and know deeply, most assuredly, with a child-like faith, that He's got it. He will gently lead me. It's what He does. He is indeed a good Father.

Jesus is again stopping me in my tracks right now, asking me to invite you into something...

We miss God's voice. God made us emotional beings, and so He speaks to us through our emotions. This may sound heretical depending on how you were raised...hang with me for a minute. It's *how* we integrate our feelings as we listen to His voice that is the crux of the matter.

I was raised in the church. I can easily write a book filled with head knowledge of who He is and how He has applied the truth of who He is into my story. This is all good and powerful. But learning, in the moment, to distinguish His voice from the voice of the enemy is one of the most life-giving and freeing lessons I could make space for in this book. As you journey towards Jesus, there will be spiritual warfare. And so, following His prompting in this very moment, I am going to walk through what He has taught me–how to discern which voice to heed as I heal and learn to walk in full surrender.

1. God tends to speak with gentle leadings in contrast to what I often perceive to be the compulsive, clamoring, loud demands of self or Satan (1 Kings 19:11-13).
2. God's voice produces freedom. Self's or Satan's voice often produces fear and bondage (2 Timothy 1:7; Matthew 11:28-30).
3. God often speaks when we are consciously seeking Him. Self or Satan often speak with sudden intrusions of thoughts into the mind (Jeremiah 29:12-13).
4. When God speaks, there is a definite sense that everything is under control. When self or Satan speak there is an inner sense that something is out of control (Psalm 46:10; Psalm 37:4).

5. God gives clear-cut, specific directions. Self or Satan often communicate in confused, uncertain wonderings. (1 Corinthians 14:33)
6. God convicts of specific sins. Self and Satan often accuse in broad generalities that leave a lingering sense of haunting and unfocused guilt (John 16:8).
7. God speaks with 100% truth that can be tested by the Word of God. Self and Satan often traffic in lies, deceit, and half-truths (John 14:6).
8. God's voice always leads to a deep, abiding sense of peace. Self often does not and Satan certainly does not. (Philippians 4:7).
9. God's voice is testable and confirmed by the wisdom of many counselors (1 John 4:1; Proverbs 11:14; Deuteronomy 19:15; and Matthew 18:16).[1]

Can you see the difference? What a crucial piece in the puzzle of our journey–knowing for certain when He speaks and what He is asking us to do. It has been the only factor in my being able to move forward at all. I would still be stuck in shame and condemnation if it weren't for His voice leading me to freedom. And now, I regularly advocate for the freedom of others. He'll do it in you too, if you seek Him.

"It's a life-long journey discerning your feelings. It takes years to grow in maturity and know what are the feelings I need to follow because they are leading me to God, and what are the feelings I am not to follow. Family of origin plays into this. If the

family you grew up in runs from conflict, then your tendency will be to do the same. But as you grow you can discern that those feelings are not ones to follow. That's not God's voice. This is why community is so important. It's not a free-for-all, we are following Jesus."

–Pete Scazerro

That night in the walk-in closet revealed so many red flags that should have sent me running for the nearest landline to call my mom to come get me. I found out this guy was 21 years old…but it flattered me all the more that an older guy would choose me. He said he was paroled over from California (we lived in Arizona) on charges of second-degree murder… complicated, I thought, but nothing Jesus couldn't fix. To say I oversimplified the situation is a gross understatement.

I shared the gospel with him that night as he convinced me to leave with him so we could hang out and "get to know one another". My level of trust when it came to people was pretty wide open. Some of it was my age–just 14, after all. I was still a child in so many ways. It was at the tender age of six that I stepped into a personal relationship with Jesus, and my understanding of who He was and who I was in Him had never been seriously tested until then.

"But he who enters by the door is the shepherd of the sheep. To him the gatekeeper opens. The sheep hear His voice, and He calls His own sheep by name and leads them out. When He has brought out all His own, He goes before them, and the sheep follow Him, for they know His voice. A stranger they will not follow, but they will flee from him, for they do not know the voice of strangers." –John 10:2-5

As we drove to one of his "friend's" houses, I remember feeling a rush of emotions, but the surface conversation he kept initiating quieted my apprehensiveness. I noted how easy he was to talk to. *"He seems genuine. He just needs someone to see past his mistakes and to give him a chance,"* I ignorantly yet hopefully spoon-fed my overstimulated conscience.

When we arrived at the home–about twenty minutes from where the rest of my volleyball team was staying the night–we went inside, past the people in the main area, into a large back bedroom. The house looked normal, as did the people. Although the neighborhood was unfamiliar to me, it felt safe. But my calming observations were abruptly interrupted.

He began pressuring me to have sex with him. He asked me several times that night alone. He was never forceful or mean. I had no desire whatsoever to lose my virginity and told him I was saving myself for marriage. And I was. *I knew God's plan for sex.*

Abstinence until marriage. And I had no intention of going against it. After several more advances, he realized I wasn't budging from my decision and took me back to the sleepover with my volleyball teammates.

I don't remember much of the rest of the night, nor do I remember any friends asking what happened or if I was okay. Perhaps they did, I just have no recollection of it. But I do remember my new friend hosting the sleepover made light of the whole ordeal after I returned. She was quick to talk about how cute this guy and I were together. Looking back, her verbiage was extremely manipulative. She tried to normalize the entire encounter and encouraged me to see him again.

"And your ears shall hear a word behind you, saying, 'This is the way, walk in it,' when you turn to the right or when you turn to the left." —Isaiah 30:21

The Victims

In the Guardian Group's 2021 report, their research shows that every victim of sex trafficking has their own unique story of exploitation. How one became a victim, what tactics their trafficker used to control them, and their recovery story are all their own.

With that in mind, the information shared below are the most common trends and patterns that are seen amongst victims of this crime. However, please remember just because someone does not fall into one of these risk categories does not make them immune.

- The average age of entry into the sex trade is 15 years-old, with 1 in 6 being under the age of 12 years-old.
- Of the federally prosecuted sex trafficking cases in 2019, only 2.1% of the victims were males.
- 42% of survivors report being placed in the foster care system.
- 61% of victims were asked to recruit other girls for their trafficker.[2]

CHAPTER 4

WORTH YOUR TRUST

Long before I even really knew God was working on my behalf, *He was*. Now, of course, I can look back and see how He was sending people at specific times, in specific places, to say or do something–like He was throwing up red flags to get me to stop and pause, to really think about the danger I was in. Although I didn't pause or stop to think things through, looking back and seeing that He was indeed providing opportunities for me to do so changed my frame of reference when trying to figure out how I could possibly trust God with hard things moving forward. *He was pursuing me*.

Understanding who He has been in the past builds our faith as we grapple with the present and look to an unknown future because we have some handles on how He showed up when it really mattered. Regardless of our response to Him truly being who He says He is, *He still is*. And the truth of this holds the power to change absolutely everything.

My first memory of Jesus pursuing me in the thick of it all was when a friend I asked to drop me off at the apartment spoke up before I got out of the car: *"Crystal, I really don't feel comfortable dropping you off here."* He told me he didn't think it was safe. I, of course, told him that I would be fine–that I knew these people, had been there before, and not to worry.

After doing some research, I know why my friend sensed danger. This apartment building was what's known as a *brothel.* These establishments may be apartments, houses, trailers, or any facility where sex is sold on the premises. It could be in a rural area or nice neighborhood. My friend obviously saw something that I did not. Looking back, I can plainly see how Jesus was transcending that moment and trying to keep me from getting out of the car. I will share more on this part of the story later, but I am so grateful for how He was reaching out to me in the midst of confusion.

There was another time after the bulk of the abuse was over, when I was sitting in my room in complete darkness. I did this a lot. I was in despair, feeling that I had ruined my life, and questioning my reason for living. I remember my mom coming in and turning on the light, saying, *"It's not good for you to sit in the dark."* Then, flipping the bright overhead light on she said, *"You need to have the light on. I'm not sure what's going on with you, Crystal, but you can't sit in the dark."*

Looking back, those words were an invitation. It was like Jesus was drawing me away from darkness toward the light. But her words also served as a stern warning. My mom knew something was wrong, but didn't know how else to encourage me forward or how to even get into the heart of what was going on, other than just encouraging me to be in a light-filled space. She knew that just sitting for hours in the dark was not good, and that it was indicative of deeper troubles waging war within me. With Jesus now guiding me back through these difficult moments, I can see how He was making space–both during and immediately after the abuse–for me to walk in the freedom that is His truth and light.

About a decade ago, just three years after opening up with my youth group girls, I felt Jesus again asking me to share my story for His purposes. I was terrified. *Still.* But it felt different as I thought about my story, this time from a bird's-eye view. I wasn't honing in on any specific details. I had just read 2 Corinthians 12:9-10, where the apostle Paul is talking about his weaknesses. He had endured so many trials in his life. They were undoubtedly traumatic experiences–being shipwrecked, wrongfully thrown into jail, beaten, and then being misunderstood over and over again while in the midst of his hardships.

In this passage he is specifically writing about a thorn in the flesh brought on by a messenger of Satan, which God permitted. The fact is, the devil is always trying to knock us down, intimidate us, and enslave us when we choose to walk in freedom with Jesus, as we turn away from all we once thought satisfied us and gave us worth. But sometimes humbling circumstances are what God chooses so that we don't become *our own enemy* through conceit and pride.

Paul says he pleaded with Jesus to take away this "thorn in the flesh," but Jesus responded, *"My grace is sufficient for you, for My power is made perfect in weakness."* (2 Corinthians 12:9a) Paul immediately understood this. *Deeply.* So much so that it changed what he asked for. He knew that apart from this "thorn," he would appear conceited and point other people to himself. So he responds from a place of humility, and in an act of surrendering his understanding for God's, he says, *"Therefore I will boast all the more gladly of my weaknesses, so that the power of Christ may rest upon me. For the sake of Christ, then, I am content with weaknesses, insults, hardships, persecutions, and calamities. For when I am weak, then I am strong."* (2 Corinthians 12:9b-10)

Paul knew that it was through a direct attack from the enemy in his life that the power of Christ would only be *more* magnified. After hearing from God Himself, Paul understood that apart from this perpetual attack, he and others would merely boast in *his* accomplishments. Paul knew that leading from a place of knowing a lot of things about God wasn't going to bring souls to salvation and free the captives. Instead, Paul embraced the truth that it was Jesus proving Himself worthy through all the hard in Paul's own life, as he struggled in real time.

This, Paul knew, would transcend the hearts of others who were also suffering and in need of a Savior.

It was upon reading this I realized that God was asking me to also surrender my brokenness for His glory so that *His strength would be seen through it.* Hiding away the most despairing parts of my story did not make me *more* worthy of God's love and favor, nor did it draw others in to know how God was proving worthy of my trust. Refusing to surrender the hard stuff (out of fear, but nonetheless) was just me putting up a Christian front, hiding behind the mere appearance of what I thought a Christ-follower ought to look like.

But my brokenness? It serves as a stark contrast and provides the very backdrop to God's redemptive work! Apart from my brokenness, I am only offering a view of *myself.* And you are too. Why wouldn't we offer *everything* up to Him as a sacrifice of praise for what He can and will do with all that threatens our physical, mental, emotional, and spiritual welfare?

God asked me to trust Him with my brokenness in stepping out to share my story. I sensed deeply that He had such a bigger plan for it all than what I could ever imagine. And so, *I surrendered.* Then, He began to build my trust in Him by actually meeting me every step of the way. I started to heal through authentically experiencing Him and sharing my story–*for His glory.*

"You've got to admit you're broken before you can be made whole."

–Lecrae

As He was drawing me out to invite others into places that had long been in darkness, He tenderly met me in the responses of my brothers and sisters in Christ. I wasn't expecting that grace. Remember, I *really* believed that Chris would be fired from his pastoral position and that we would be kicked out of the church. So to have people respond with compassion, sympathy and grace astounded me. I had never even pictured God reacting to my whole story in this way, let alone imperfect fellow humans. I learned so much about God's character through watching how His people responded to my trauma, and God just brought more healing through it.

It was so simple. He asked me to step out in faith, and then He gently built my trust each step of the way. I never really knew what the next step was going to be each time I was asked to surrender. But by leaning into His grace in the present moment, learning to distinguish His voice apart from the voice of the masses, and apart from the voice of the enemy, He grew my trust in Him. And then, just when I needed it, the next step appeared. More faith was required. And I took the step. I am more and more assured today than ever before that He will meet me as I step out into unknown spaces.

Now, this doesn't make taking steps of faith any easier. Actually, the stakes seem higher the longer I journey with Him. Perhaps they've always been high–maybe I can just see the weight of the steps I take now compared to the past. But I can tell you one thing: reckless abandon to all that holds me back feels *so good and necessary*. Kind of like cliff jumping into unfamiliar waters, but with the most capable and loving Guide there to meet you where your understanding comes to an end and faith takes hold of your fears, with His tender grace enveloping you as you journey into places you've never been before.

"Our discipleship needs to incorporate every aspect of our humanity (mind, body, emotion, spirit). Doctrine is great to study, but we really cannot know Scripture without feeling. When it's all head and it's not heart, it's a tragedy."

–Pete Scazerro

As I journey towards His heart, I feel my confidence secured in who He is when He calls me out. I know His voice increasingly more by the day. And what's more, I know that I can trust Him because every time He has called me out He has never once abandoned me. He always meets me and supplies everything I need to do what He's calling me to do. I am more certain of this truth than ever before.

So please, Lord Jesus…Your Kingdom come, Your will be done.

To the Young Girl Trapped in Darkness…

It's difficult for me to speak to the young girl who's currently enslaved. In so many ways, I feel like I'm speaking to my younger self, and there's still so much of that space that needs healed in me. It feels raw and vulnerable.

If given the opportunity though, I would hold her hand, look her in the eyes, and offer some tear-filled, humble words of encouragement. I would tell her to pull away from the situation, to get in a space where she can be *still*–somewhere away from the predominant voices in her life. I would encourage her to lean into spaces where there are people who love her sacrificially and who love God wholly. I would tell her to be brave enough to ask the hard questions. *I would tell her to be brave enough to invite people into her reality.*

Even as I write this, I know that *I wasn't brave enough to do that.* I had zero awareness of the danger I was in. I thought I had a handle on it, and no one could tell me otherwise. I was completely and utterly lost in a world of fake love, fake promises, and fake security.

But there were safe places for me as a teenager–pockets of grace that God had created for me. I just didn't lean into them. My home was safe. My Mom kept making space for me to open up to her. Although she worked crazy long hours, I knew she would always make time for me. It seemed to me as a young girl that my Dad's mission in life was to keep his girls safe. His experiences—from Vietnam to working the graveyard shift as a security guard in dangerous parts of South Phoenix to being a trophy-winning competition shooter—made me certain he would do whatever was necessary to ensure my physical safety.

I also had a pastor's wife, with whom I could have had a real conversation, amid all this. She would have been a most gracious listener and friend.

God had these people there in my life for a purpose. Of course, I can see that now, but seeking help from any of them wasn't an option in my mind. At the time, I believed none of these people would have accepted me, nor could they provide what I believed I needed. At the time, I believed my worth came from my 21-year-old "boyfriend". And I knew all these people would tell me he wasn't good for me. If they found out about our relationship, they would have made sure we never saw one another again. Tragically, the very person I believed I needed more than anyone was someone positioning himself to *exploit me.*

To the Parent/Friend/Ministry Leader

Are you the concerned mom or dad? What about the friend seeing warning signs or red flags? Maybe you're the pastor's wife, ministry leader, or small group leader. What questions could you ask to draw out the heart of that person who needs a lifeline right now? Perhaps you sense that mere words and Bible verses will only push them further away. What does it look like for you to consistently make a safe space for them? What does it look like to embody Jesus in their life?

Here's the deal. The enemy wants you to believe that either the weight of changing this person is entirely on your shoulders, or that you don't have what it takes to make a difference in their life. *You must make it happen...but you aren't enough.* Both are lies meant to crowd out the voice and diminish the power of Jesus in and through you.

Get into the Word of God. *Regularly.* Be a man or woman of the Word. Let it radically transform you from the inside out. PRAY for your heart to move together with His, and then *pray* for your loved one's salvation from slavery. Be proactive in making space for them to open up. Tell them you love them and that you're here for them. Let them know you're fighting for them to understand where their identity comes from. Do it all from a place of gentleness, not condemnation.

Don't give up. They need someone whose love is unconditional to step into the ring with them. They must see Jesus *in you*! And you can trust that His power, through your surrender and dependence on

Him, is more than enough. Transformation is *His work*. And it is done in *His timing*. But He uses us as the conduits through which freedom is extended, over and over again, to those who are enslaved in darkness.

Grooming, as explained by Guardian Group, "is the stage when a pimp builds a relationship with their victim, gains their trust and oftentimes make an emotional connection. This allows the pimp to manipulate and control the victim better in the future. There is no single form of force, fraud or coercion used by predators, as each trafficker has their own style to gain the necessary power and control required to manipulate an individual into doing what they want.

85% of victims reported developing a close relationship with their trafficker.

This close relationship statistic portrays the Romeo Pimp tactic of manipulating and nurturing a relationship with their victim. The Romeo Pimp will manipulate their victim into believing they are truly in a romantic relationship, as this is done by buying them gifts, taking them out to eat and spoiling them in some form. This tactic creates a bond between the victim and the trafficker and often the victim believes they are selling themselves because it is how they contribute to the relationship. Forty-two percent of victims report their trafficker earned their trust within one month of meeting, while another 28% report the trafficker earned their trust within four months."

I am not a professional when it comes to trafficking terms, but it seems to me that my "boyfriend" was a temporary lure that my pimp used to bring in teenage girls. *That was hard to type.* I physically paused after typing "my" before the word "pimp". Whatever my 14-year-old-self thought she was getting into, it certainly wasn't this. This pimp was not *mine*–but he was working in the darkness to ensure that I was *his*.

We want to echo God's truth and love to those who are suffering and desperately searching for meaning and worth. We can't do it alone. But God can shine His redeeming light into the darkest places *through us*. Hope, wisdom, and freedom are never out of reach–they can always be found in Jesus. If you haven't already, commit yourself to healing from *your own past hurts*. Then you can be a safe space for someone else. Otherwise, the very same lies the enemy has used to keep you bound for years will seep through your words and actions as you attempt to help others. We aren't meant to pour our broken selves into others. Rather, Jesus pours out *through our brokenness*.

There's a lie the enemy has used to enslave generations: *that brokenness is somehow a sin*. Pride blinds people to their own slavery and demands that others "walk the line" or be condemned. In the Bible, these were the Pharisees and Sadducees. They were all about pious beliefs and lofty appearances, but their hearts were far from God. The fruit of their labor was devastation for the hurting and needy.

But who did Jesus choose to perform miracles among? The broken. The despised. The rejected. Those who were viewed as "dysfunctional" by the ones merely playing religion. Jesus drew near to them because *they knew* they needed Him. There was no doubt in their minds that, unless Jesus moved, there would be no hope.

Praise God, Jesus did move! And He still moves among us today through His Spirit, offering forgiveness to sinners, with healing and hope for the broken and discarded. *But whose voice will you echo to a hurting world?*

"Emotions aren't wrong, they are necessary. You cannot have deep relationships or solve conflict if you aren't intentional in growing emotionally. 'I can't enter your world because I can't enter mine.'"

–Pete Scazerro

If you want a better future, start by working on your emotional health. Since I am a mama of three precious souls, my mind goes to them. My healing journey impacts them–and my husband–profoundly. Stop and think about this for a moment: emotionally unhealthy parents cannot be what their children need them to be, and so their children grow up to be unstable adults as well. Of course, God's grace and redemption have the final word on who someone becomes. He can intervene and change the trajectory of anyone's life at any time. But you can't sit back and let the lies that have enslaved you for years continue to do so if you desire healthy relationships. If you're a parent, it's never too late to apologize to your children. Tell them you now realize how your emotional state has impacted them negatively. Whether they are still in the home or are out on their own, the healing that can come from offering your child space to be understood cannot be overstated. Let them express what it's been like living under your emotional instability. *Sound daunting?* Jesus is worth your trust. He is the Author of restoration stories, and He's not done with your story yet.

Now, it's possible that *you* were raised by emotionally unhealthy parents. Regardless of how they are–or were–perceived in the public eye, they were not the parents you needed them to be. *But you can stop the cycle.* Pray and ask Jesus what the next step is. Seek some solid Christian counseling so you can begin to heal. Then, get a handle on the hurt you've caused others. This is how Jesus redeems generations–it can start with you. Don't you want to be remembered for the life you *gave*, rather than for the life you *took away*?

Jesus sees you. There's so much more to relationships than you've ever known. And there are no shortcuts. You simply must *do the hard work.* But remember,

Jesus does the heavy lifting. We aren't promised tomorrow. Today's the day. Let's do it together.

In highschool, I had a pager–or "beeper," as we cool kids called it–and it was the only way to communicate without using the landline. This was 1996, so the landline was our only option other than payphones. If you had more than one phone in the house, which we did, anyone could pick up the other phone and listen to the entire conversation. So, my "boyfriend" and I sent coded messages back and forth via my beeper, and we planned for our next meet up.

Social Media Sites Have Allowed Traffickers A Faster, Simpler and More Effective Mechanism to Recruit Victims

Guardian Group shares a stark warning in their 2021 Report on Sex Trafficking in America. "The amount of information we freely offer to the world about ourselves makes it easier for traffickers to find their next victim without ever leaving the couch. Predators troll the social sites to try and spot vulnerabilities. They are good at it. A statement such as "my parents are the worst" or "I'm so over school" allows the predator to connect, relate and offer comfort and a solution to the victim. Some predators send out a hundred direct messages a day just hoping for a handful of responses. These messages might include something along the lines of "wow you are beautiful" or "I have a problem...can you help me?"

By instilling confidence in our young people we can start to protect them from the predators that recruit in-person. Things like making eye contact, keeping your head up and being direct when you speak are all deterrents to a trafficker. In the online space, teaching a young person to never post their frustrations or their heart on the internet will make them less of a target. Also the importance of bringing messages sent from strangers to a trusted adult instead of responding allows the message to be reported and the young person to be protected."[1]

CHAPTER 5

HE DELIGHTS IN PROVING IT

Jesus is worthy of our trust, and He will prove it–not because He must, but because He's after our whole heart. He is gentle and patient with His own. These attributes of God can be bypassed in a church culture that demands you come presentable to God. But this is not the heart of our tender Father. Jesus is the One who makes us presentable by His finished work on the cross. Why does this matter? Because if God is the former, demanding my put-togetherness, I would never bring my hurt, frustration, trauma, and fears to Him. But if God is the latter, I would bring my everything to Him, trusting that He knows exactly what to do with my shortcomings.

Grace is often defined as undeserved favor (Ephesians 2:8). It is the very quality in God that gives gifts to undeserving sinners. It's free. It's undeserved. But grace is also a power for obedience. (2 Corinthians 12:9, 1 Corinthians 15:10) Grace works in us to change our capacity for work, suffering, and obedience. It is more than a character trait. Grace is also the action, power, influence, and force which produces practical outcomes in people's lives. It is help where we need it.[1]

"Let us with confidence, draw near to the throne of grace, that we may receive mercy and find grace to help in time of need."
—Hebrews 4:16

When we view our suffering through the lens of His grace, we can see that God comes alongside us and helps us get where we need to be, building up our trust in Him with each step of our healing journey. It's a gentle, compassionate response to whatever emotions we bring to Him. He doesn't ask us to put ourselves together; His are the hands that do that sanctifying work.

I love the way Dr. Paul David Tripp talks about grace. He explains that God's grace makes our stories *instruments of work* within His kingdom. God knows how confident we can be in our own strength. So, He will take us where we haven't intended to go in order to produce in us what we could not achieve on our own. The Bible calls this grace.[2]

I was in Bible college the first time I heard the story of the refiner's fire. Refining gold by fire is one of the oldest methods of refining metals and is mentioned in the Bible. In ancient times, gold refiners would sit next to a hot fire, stirring and skimming the molten gold to remove impurities. Newly mined gold has fragments in it that would compromise its strength and purity if not removed. So, the blacksmith increases the heat of the fire, causing the gold to become liquid and sink to the bottom, while the impurities within the gold to rise to the surface, where the blacksmith can skim them away. The blacksmith repeats these steps until he can see his reflection on the surface of the gold.

This visual has stuck with me through every trial and helps me lean in amidst the discomfort. Anger, frustration, fear, doubt, shame, condemnation, inadequacy–let them come to the surface *through hardships* so that He can lovingly skim them away. Impurities are within us, without a doubt. Jesus knows this, and He won't settle for less than us being made into His image. He loves us too much to allow the things that leave us vulnerable to the enemy's attacks to linger.

As we heal, uncomfortable memories and feelings are brought to the surface–but not without purpose. Jesus knows just what to do with them and can be trusted as our Master Refiner. He faithfully skims away the impurities and will continue to do so until He can see His image in us.

In Jesus' redemptive and loving hands, our hurt is turned to healing.

For years, I didn't bring my trauma to God. I kept it hidden away. I knew I couldn't hide it from God, but truth be told, I didn't think I could bear His reaction to my darkness, so I tucked it away. I believed I deserved my abuse. I thought that because I lied to my parents about where I was going and who I would be with, He sent bad people to do horrible things to me. A perfect God cannot tolerate sin in His presence–which is true. There are consequences for our sins–also true. A just God demands punishment for sins. *Punishment though? Even for those who are His?*

Punishment is imposing a penalty on someone for something they did. It makes someone pay a price for what they did. But here's the thing: *God does not punish His children. He does discipline us*. Discipline is intended to drive out unhealthy behaviors from our lives. (Proverbs 3:12; Hebrews 12:6)

The difference between God's discipline of His children and His punishment of His enemies is an infinite one. God's judgment of His enemies is meant solely to express His holy justice–His retribution, not restitution. No mercy is demonstrated here (Revelation 16:5-6). The guilty deserve this justice because of their sin. *It is not designed for rehabilitation*. On the other hand, God's discipline of His children is vastly different (Hebrews 12:5-11).[3] We are loved as sons and daughters, and discipline is the act of bringing us back to His heart for our good, so we can share in His holiness. Temporary discomfort brought on because of our own sin may bring His discipline, but it's meant to produce eternal righteousness.

So, let's get back to the question at hand: did God send evil men to hurt me as a punishment because I lied to my parents? *No, He did not.*

Paul Tripp points out that grace never calls *wrong* right. Sin is sin, and it needs God's forgiveness and transformative power. My lying was sinful. But we can't apply the law *without grace*, because it would beat us down and cause us to believe things that just aren't true about how God views us in our sin, as I falsely believed in my story. As His sons and daughters, the law is meant to *drive us towards grace*. If God's only function is as a judge, who in the world is going to run towards Him? He is faithful, gracious, and understanding, *never turning His back* on His own.[4]

I will continue to break this down throughout the book, because it's crucial that we understand God's posture towards us. *The redemption of our stories is at stake.*

God delights in those who reverence Him, trust Him, and put their hope in His unfailing love. He does not delight in strength, but He delights in us when we acknowledge our weakness and our need of Him (Psalm 147:11).

If we cannot ask hard questions of God we will never fully be able to trust Him with the things that matter most to us. We may be able to go through the motions of Christianity, but when things outside of our control enter into our reality, the house we hurriedly constructed on a faulty foundation *will crumble*. When we perpetually fail to get a handle on what's in front of us, we isolate, medicate, and self-soothe just to survive. It's a desperate existence, and we settle for it time and time again because facing our brokenness head-on is impossible without the certainty that we can trust God. His grace meets us where we are and takes us where we need to go.

So go there with Jesus. Ask Him the hard questions about your story. There may be things you're believing that are unnecessarily beating you down and keeping you from seeking Him to begin your healing journey.

In those first couple of weeks, my boyfriend would pick me up immediately after school. There was some free time each day when I normally hung out in the NJROTC room with my friends, and my parents knew this was where they could find me after school. I had never given them a reason to think otherwise. I wasn't the kid that went looking for trouble, but trouble had indeed found me.

Honestly, much of what we did together during those first weeks is a blur. What I do remember is him introducing me to other men. Lots of them. One time, he and a bunch of his friends were in an alley of sorts smoking marijuana. He kept trying to get me to take a hit. I politely refused, mentally chalking it up as one more thing Jesus needed to help my boyfriend give up. He blew the smoke in my face and laughed, as did his friends. I held my breath for as long as I could, trying hard not to make it obvious, so I could seem like I had things under control. But every single time we were together, he pressured me to have sex with him. He was never violent, he just kept applying relentless pressure.

After just a week, he told me he loved me. *Is this what love feels like?* I remember thinking it was pretty lackluster and odd to say it so soon and in a gas station parking lot nonetheless. But after a few seconds of shock and disbelief, I responded, "I love you too." And I convinced myself I did. It was a choice made based on where I believed my worth came from. This man I hardly knew standing in front of me…he said I was beautiful. Surely, no other man thought so. I had to hang on to this one.

One day soon after, he took me to an apartment complex in my hometown. It was quaint with only four units, two on the ground level and two above. We walked up the stairs to the apartment on the top floor to the right. It was around 3pm on a weekday, so I was surprised when we walked in to find two men and a woman already there. They were noticeably older–in their 30s. I wasn't good at discerning age, everyone was "old" to me back then, but I knew they looked old enough to be my parents.

He introduced me to his two "uncles." The name of the one escapes me, or perhaps my memory has buried it deep enough that I just can't access it anymore. I don't remember a time when he was there that he wasn't making disgusting sexual advances at me. He was crude and disrespectful to both me and the woman sitting next to him. She never spoke or made eye contact with anyone. She was like a shell of a woman. It was like she was someone's…property.

"What's her name again?" I always asked my boyfriend.

"Who?" he responded.

"Your uncle's wife," I said. I was always trying to fit what I saw and experienced into a Christian framework. He told me her name a few different times. I feel so badly for forgetting it. Her face and countenance are still etched in my mind, though, connected to a deep sense of despair. It was like she wanted to be seen but couldn't ask for attention. *She had no voice*. No opinion. No will of her own. All of this my young mind grasped deeply. It was hard to look away. I can't think of that apartment without thinking of her.

Reckless Eyeballing - term which refers to the act of looking around instead of keeping your eyes on the ground. Eyeballing is against the rules and could lead an untrained victim to "choose up" by mistake. This was why the woman who often sat next to the more domineering "uncle" (pimp) never made eye contact or spoke. It breaks my heart just thinking about her. I hope and pray with all my heart that she found freedom, and that she is now finally safe to heal.

Choosing Up - The process by which a different pimp takes "ownership" of a victim. Victims are instructed to keep their eyes on the ground at all times. According to traditional pimping rules, when a victim makes eye contact with another pimp (accidentally or on purpose), she is choosing him to be her pimp. If the original pimp wants the victim back, he must pay a fee to the new pimp. When this occurs, he will force the victim to work harder to replace the money lost in transaction.[5]

PART 3

EXAMINE FEAR

CHAPTER 6

IS IT A SIN TO FEAR

I couldn't stop crying. This wasn't a cry birthed in sadness, but rather my deepest fears being relived in both my waking and my sleeping moments. There was nothing I could do to escape it. I knew the verses, I prayed more heartfelt prayers than ever before in my life…and yet, that all-enslaving fear remained. After a solid week of being unable to escape the torture that accompanied the details of my past, my husband, filled with the Holy Spirit, called it out. There in the humble kitchen of the first home we ever owned, he told me that it was not Jesus I was following, but a spirit of fear.

The fruit was plain and obvious to him after having carefully examined my behavior and torment that week. In God's sovereignty, He led Chris to pursue his master's degree in Biblical Counseling, which he had nearly completed by this time. So, it was simple enough, examining the fruit of me diving into the darkest places of my story. My heart wanted to be obedient. It wanted healing. The fact was, I was ignorant of the ways the enemy would try to enslave me throughout the journey. How did I not anticipate spiritual warfare? Why was I controlled by *fear*?

Diagnosing areas in need of restoration within yourself can prove difficult, mainly because it's all you've ever known. But what if we used the fruit we can see to *help* us determine the root cause? And what if we invited help in doing so?

The gift of having a space to feel what you are feeling and not be condemned has not traditionally been part of the church. Jennie Allen, author of *Untangle Your Emotions*, has recently done much personal heart work and now teaches boldly on the matter. She says, "God has more room to work when we are not pretending, shoving down and concealing. It's the gift of walking this human journey with our human emotions, and bringing them to God and bringing them to each other, and not wasting energy pretending we are not feeling a certain way…it sets us free."

We often try to show a little emotion, but then feel the need to quickly follow up with the actions we're putting into place to combat that emotion. For example, you might share with a close friend that you're struggling with yelling at your kids–but as soon as the words leave your mouth, you immediately feel regret emotionally exposing yourself. So, you quickly follow up with, "but I'm praying about it and memorizing Scripture on anger."

Jennie says to, *"feel it, name it, share it if you need to, then decide what to do with it. Fall apart, ball your eyes out if you need to. Do what you need to do to feel that emotion. Then make a choice about what you are going to do with it. Don't let the emotion be your god. Your will drives the train, not your emotions."* Jennie is *not* suggesting we do what the world does and let ourselves be controlled by our emotions.

DO NOT conceal your emotions. You read that right. Stuffing, hiding, masking, using coping mechanisms…why do we do it? Because certain emotions have been deemed *bad* to feel. Here's the deal though–your emotions give insight into what's going on deep inside. Like a "check engine" light on your dashboard. Rewiring your car so the light turns off is like choosing not to feel your emotions–*it's not actually fixing anything.*

This is not to say that your emotions should have control over you. There is a difference. But feel what you are feeling. God made us emotional beings for a reason. *Stop trying to look the part.*

Emotions are gifts. They lead us to things in our lives we've been missing. They can take us to parts of our soul, parts of our story, that we haven't wanted to pay attention to. Sometimes we are so busy telling our brains what to feel that we miss the opportunity to let theology sink down and shape our hearts in a core way. We are often too consumed with making sure we–a*nd everyone else*–know *what* we should be thinking about our emotions, that we miss the actual transformative work Jesus would do *through* our emotions.

"Then Moses summoned Joshua and said to him in the sight of all Israel, 'Be strong and courageous, for you shall go with this people into the land that the Lord has sworn to their fathers to give them, and you shall put them in possession of it. It is the Lord who goes before you. He will be with you; He will not leave you or forsake you. Do not fear or be dismayed.'" —Deuteronomy 31:7-8

God comes alongside Joshua and offers him comfort, telling him not to fear because He will be with him. He isn't condemning Joshua for being afraid, nor is He trying to fix him. Fear in and of itself is not a sin–*it's what you do with it that matters*. When we allow fear to have control over us, we're in trouble. God alone is worthy to have control over us.

But what about PTSD? If our actual brains were altered during moments of severe trauma, do we have a choice as to whether or not fear controls us?

I explained in the beginning of the chapter how enslaved I was to fear when I attempted to work through the details of my past trauma. The moment Chris called out a spirit of fear in me, he also read Galatians 5:1 over me. He told me that I was FREE and needed to get up and walk away from the shackles that once enslaved me before I knew Christ. The image was clear. I had unknowingly allowed the details of my past to bring me right back to the slave block that once held me captive before I knew Jesus as my Savior. I wasn't yet ready to talk through the details of my trauma without submitting myself to a yoke of slavery. I didn't know *how* to heal–but Jesus began to show me.

Step by step, I was learning to recognize His tender leading. I knew the feeling within me that made my chest tighten and my body shake. It was the all-too-familiar trauma response. *Was Jesus in the details?* He absolutely was, and is. It just wasn't time in my journey for me to revisit them. Not yet.

Years have gone by, and He has walked with me through many more details of my past, giving me freedom from the grip they once had on me. Neurologically speaking, Jesus has given me the support I've needed to begin reconnecting neural pathways that were broken by trauma. As I've shared my story with others and intentionally invited Him into the parts I don't know what to do with, my brain, my emotions, and my body now have so much more capacity to live this life as He intended.

You don't know the freedom available to you until you start to work through the things you have deep down inside. When you do, you'll recognize that the coping mechanisms you had in place were robbing you of the fullness of life Jesus created you to walk in.

But you can't fix what you don't know is broken, right? God desires to restore your heart and make it stronger than ever before. I know this to be true, but my brain craved an illustration–and I found a good one!

The Japanese art of fixing what is broken is known as *Kintsugi*. It is directly translated as "golden joinery" and is the practice of repairing broken pottery with lacquer and gold.

The golden parts are the cracks where the bowl broke. *Kintsugi* considers breakage and repair as the most important part of the object's history, rather than something to hide.[1]

It's a great analogy for what Jesus does with our brokenness when we surrender it to Him. He doesn't ask us to hide our broken parts–He uses them to highlight His redemptive power so a hurting world can look at us and see that although we are broken vessels, He intricately and powerfully holds us together. Now, when He uses us, *His* work is the focal point. We are made more into His image than before the damage occurred.

Think about that for a moment…when His master work is weaved throughout the tapestry of our lives, what stands out are the times He showed up and proved that He is who He says He is! *Through our brokenness*, His light shines more brilliantly into the darkness. It's what a hurting world longs to see–something real that will offer them hope which cannot fail. A promise that their broken pieces can also be put back together, and somehow even more beautifully.

Seeking professional counseling is *finally* becoming less and less taboo within the church. And with so many great options out there, it's never been easier to get help as you sort through complicated emotions in an effort to grow and heal. But listen up, church… *we can do more*!

God actually created us to counsel one another with the Word of God, with each of our uniqueness and life experience adding special insight and compassion to those in need. Chris and I believe that most counseling can actually be done effectively and beautifully within the context of a 1:1 discipleship relationship or a small group. If you've never thought of yourself as a counselor before, this may sound overwhelming.

For those who are ready to dive in, I have included in the *appendix* of this book some of the very same tools my husband has used as a biblical soul care pastor to equip believers to do the work of the ministry that is discipleship/counseling.

What if–instead of hiding away emotions we believe, or have been told, are unfitting for Christians to feel–*we invite Jesus into them* as an act of surrender, acknowledging that He knows the way forward from where you stand today? Just like the art of *Kintsugi*, Jesus takes our brokenness and restores us in such a way that highlights His redemptive work in the broken spaces of our story. Shame is replaced with His glory, and fear has no choice but to give way to freedom as we follow His lead.

"Why didn't she say something when your uncle was talking to me like that?" I asked.

"Like what?" my boyfriend responded.

It was only then I realized he was never actually in the room when his uncle would talk to me so disgustingly. "Oh, that's just how she is" he replied. As I mentioned before, there were always two uncles sitting in that apartment. After noticing my discomfort, but definitely allowing it for a while, the other uncle in the room would speak up: "Stop talking to her like that." And the vulgar talk stopped immediately. "Uncle Mikey" positioned himself as a father figure from the very beginning. He seemed to be the one my boyfriend was endeared to in some way, and so I began to trust him too. He gave me no reason to think poorly of him. He often asked if I wanted anything to eat or drink, and was light-hearted and seemingly protective.

Family/Folks - The term used to describe the other individuals under the control of the same pimp. He plays the role of father (or "Daddy") while the group fulfills the need for a "family."[2]

In the circuit I was in, the pimps were referred to as "Uncle", at least in these beginning stages.

Pimp Circle - When several pimps encircle a victim to intimidate through verbal and physical threats in order to discipline the victim or force her to choose up. Within the first few weeks of my situation, one "Uncle" played the father figure, and the other took a much more domineering and verbally aggressive role.

A trafficker is someone who exploits another individual for their own personal gain. In the same way each victim has their own unique story, each trafficker has their own tactics for recruiting victims and maintaining control over them. Some use fear and violence, others use emotional manipulation. Traffickers may work individually or they may be a part of a gang or larger criminal network facilitating this crime.

Those who intentionally recruited minors said they did it because younger women are easier to manipulate, work harder to earn money, and are more marketable.[3]

CHAPTER 7

HOW THE PAST IS AFFECTING YOUR INTIMACY

Self-preservation mode is no place to camp out. I know because I myself have wandered in this desert land. It is in opposition to how God created us–we were designed to be intimate beings, living life vulnerably with Him and His people. If this sounds terrifying to you, *ask God why*. What has happened that causes you to guard those inner spaces of your heart from God and others? What comes to mind is your next step…let's unpack it together with God.

Denial of trauma is a defense mechanism that protects you from emotional pain. Sometimes, however, healing is on the other side of it. Confronting the traumatic event and what it means to you may bring up hurtful memories and sensations. Trauma denial may serve as a shield that emotionally and mentally disconnects you from the traumatic event, but it may not aid you in healing the pain. Trauma denial is a way to put distance between you and an overwhelming experience. But ongoing trauma denial causes more suffering than there needs to be.[1]

In an effort to suppress memories that are too painful for you to face, you block off certain portions of your heart and mind. Some of this blocking off or putting up walls is subconscious, while some of it is intentional–you do it so often it's become a rut in the road that your tires get pulled into every single time something triggers you…a certain topic, the name of someone who hurt you, a geographical location, a song, a smell, a feeling, a nightmare that replays the trauma.

Let's focus for a moment on the part that you can work through–the cognizant pushing away or stuffing of difficult feelings that arise. Remember, in Christ we are not victims but more than conquerors (Romans 8:37). What would happen if, instead of pushing away, *you leaned in*? How could things change if you simply asked Jesus for help when you feel overwhelmed? The moment you notice your body reacting to a memory, thought, or conversation, who could you tell? Simply share with a trusted friend, "I had a physical reaction when _______ happened. I don't know why yet, but I need someone that I trust to know."

The enemy wants us to believe we are alone, and that it would bring shame upon us if anyone found out about our inner struggles. But this is a bold-faced lie. Reject it by memorizing this truth:

"There is therefore now no condemnation for those who are in Christ Jesus. For the law of the Spirit of life has set you free in Christ Jesus from the law of sin and death." –Romans 8:1-2

We are not going to grow in all the ways we need to overnight. But step by step, we heal. Day by day, we are made more into the image of Jesus Christ, who personally knows our sufferings. Man of sorrows, despised and rejected, broken and bruised *for us*. Good news… Jesus is in the work of healing and redemption (Isaiah 53). He is worth our trust as we lean into things too great for us to bear, because He bore it all on our behalf.

I have always been a people person. From a young age, I engaged freely with adults and children alike, never shying away from an opportunity to connect in conversation or activity. I really didn't know a stranger. During holidays, when the extended family gathered together, I was often found conversing with an aunt or an uncle about the weather, hobbies, or decorations. I loved cousin time, and was always up for a game of Old Maid or tag in the front yard.

From grade school through high school, I was known as "the church hugger," as I went row to row, hugging and briefly visiting with each attender, whether I knew them or not. We always attended smaller churches, so it was an easy goal to accomplish each Sunday.

After the traumatic experiences in my high school years, I pulled away, but not enough for most people to notice. I was still considered out-going and kind, a friend to most. But I can look back and see how I was guarded, only allowing people in so far. I became good at putting walls up in a way that wasn't intrusive or noticeable in my everyday relationships. I wasn't mean to people, I just changed the subject if things were uncomfortable, or I would stop talking altogether.

It wasn't until after I was married that I could see a portion of my heart was closed off. There is no human relationship more intimate than that of a husband and wife. As we began to live out our commitment to becoming one–household and in flesh–my poor efforts to preserve myself were exposed. For the first time, I couldn't hide from the effects of trauma holding me captive in mind, body, and soul.

I became especially aware of it when we were physically intimate. Every emotion intermingled in one confusing, tangled mess. But Chris didn't have this kind of trauma in his past, so I remember deciding not to talk to him about it. *"It's my problem. Chris shouldn't have to deal with it. If I just stuff it further down it will go away, as if it never happened. I am a different person than I was then."*

The reality was that the Spirit of God was trying to bring to light what was not meant to be hidden away in darkness. I blamed myself for the abuse. *"I should have never lied to my parents about where I was going and who I would be with,"* I thought. Up went a wall every time we were physically intimate.

Because neither of us grew up in families or churches where physical intimacy was talked about–except in a "don't have sex before marriage" kind of way–we weren't naturally inclined to talk about the disconnect we both noticed. Up went another wall in emotional intimacy with my husband.

I believed God to be a judge who was angry at me for putting myself in the position to be abused. *"I was supposed to be set apart from the world. Why did I ever think I could handle the situation?? God is distant and mad at me."* Up went another wall in spiritual intimacy with God, who I had completely misunderstood, by the way. More on His character later, but He is a very good God, tender and ever-present in our time of need. Boy, did the enemy have me confused.

I was *dissociating*, and it became my default when I felt threatened. Instead of leaning into areas that needed healing, in the context of a loving relationship with a wonderful husband and an amazing God, I cut off anything that awakened the memories I so desperately wanted to escape.

The problem is, *everything is connected*. God made us to be intimately connected to Him and His creation–to engage deeply with our Creator and others. To share in the carrying of loads too burdensome for us to bear on our own. I wasn't living life; I was spending most of my energy managing and covering up symptoms of the wreckage from my past.

Dissociation is one way the mind copes with too much stress, such as during a traumatic event. You may feel detached from your body, or feel as though the world around you is unreal. PTSD will cause you to continue disconnecting long after the traumatic event(s) are over through emotions brought on by "triggers"–which is anything that reminds you of your trauma. When triggers make you feel as if you're reliving parts of your trauma, this is known as a "flashback". Dissociation can range from mild emotional detachment to severe disconnection from physical and emotional experiences.

Now that we have the definitions out of the way, hear this: you do not *have* to disconnect from the people you love and from the world you live in. It is not God's heart for you moving forward. There is another way. There is healing. There is real hope.

I remember the first time I experienced Jesus in a worship setting as a grown adult. Crazy enough, it was ten years into ministry! I guess when you grow up in the church, you can sing songs about who God is without really letting them sink in. They are just words you sing. Every Sunday. First, second, and fourth stanzas. Apart from *As the Deer* and *Refiner's Fire* sang around the campfire at the end of a Spirit-filled message from a gifted youth speaker, I can remember no other connections with God through worship on a heart level up until this point in my Christian life. *Crazy*.

Back to the story: it was the words, the atmosphere, a room full of fellow believers expectant for God to show up and transform lives. It was the young man in front of me who couldn't hold it together, surrounded by his small group as they all cried out to God because his wife had just walked out on him. It all made me very aware of how paper-thin my emotions felt. I couldn't run from God any longer. He had been chasing me down, and I had nowhere left to go. I was surrounded by His goodness, grace, and promises of redemption for the very things I'd spent what seemed like a lifetime trying to hide.

"I trust You, Jesus. I don't know how, but I trust You in this moment. But if I sing these words out loud I won't be able to hold back the tears...the whole world will know I am broken too. Are pastor's wives even allowed to be broken?! Do You really know what You are asking of me, Jesus?? We could lose it all...our position in ministry, our friends, our livelihood...it's all here within these walls."

He tenderly responded, *"I see you, Crystal. I see every detail. Nothing is hidden from me. I created you to be a window into the real-time work I am doing in your heart and life, not a door that shuts everyone out. I know you don't know what to expect. I know you are full of fear. But you can trust Me. Sing the words, Crystal. Let the tears come, and let others see how I am proving in real time to be the very God I say I am."*

Not For A Moment

by Meredith Andrews[2]

(used with Meredith Andrews' permission)

You were reaching through the storm
Walking on the water
Even when I could not see
In the middle of it all
When I thought You were a thousand
Miles away
Not for a moment
Did You forsake me
Not for a moment
Did You forsake me

You were singing in the dark
Whispering Your promise
Even when I could not hear
I was held in Your arms
Carried for a thousand miles to show
Not for a moment did You forsake me
Not for a moment did You forsake me

[Chorus]
And after all, You are constant
After all, You are only good
After all, You are sovereign
Not for a moment did You forsake me
Not for a moment will You forsake me

[Bridge]
And every step, every breath, You are there

Every tear, every cry, every prayer
In my hurt, at my worst,
when my world falls down
Not for a moment will You forsake me
Not for a moment will You forsake me

[Chorus]
After all, You are constant
Yes, after all, You are only good
After all, You are sovereign
Not for a moment will You forsake me
Not for a moment will You forsake me
After all, You are constant
After all, You are only good
After all, You are sovereign
Not for a moment will You forsake me
Not for a moment will You forsake me

I was sleeping soundly, when I heard a knock on my bedroom window. My bedroom was located in the front of the house, next to the driveway. Startled, I jumped out of bed and barely lifted my blinds. It was my boyfriend. *What in the world is he doing here?*

I cracked open my window, and we spoke in a whisper, to avoid waking the rest of my family. "Come out with me," he pleaded, "just for a little bit." He assured me he would have me back before anyone woke up and that it would be okay. "Okay, I'll be out in a minute," I whispered, closing the window.

I turned to change out of my pajamas and grab a sweater. I felt an immense conflict within me at that moment. Looking back, I know it was the Holy Spirit pleading with me not to go. But my fear of losing the only man who thought I was beautiful was greater than my fear of God. And so I left with him.

We drove only two streets over from my house, maybe just three or four blocks away. We pulled up to a dark, brick, one-story ranch that looked like no one was home. There was a chain-link fence around the yard, just like most houses in the area. My boyfriend got out of the car and opened the gate. We pulled into the driveway as he closed the gate behind us…it felt like the responsible, safe thing to do. My mom and dad always closed the gate behind us after we pulled the cars in for the night.

He opened the front door, and, holding my hand in his, we walked in. There were no lights on in the house except for a single lamp in a back bedroom. The path from the front door to the bedroom was straight. As we walked toward the light, I noticed the house was empty.

"This is my friend's house. He's in the middle of moving," he said. As we made our way into the bedroom, I noticed only two other things apart from the lamp: an AM/FM radio with a cassette player, and a mattress on a box spring lying directly on the floor. No frame, no actual bedding– just a single, unfitted white sheet draped over the mattress.

He hit play on the cassette player. It was our song. Walmart sold single hits for $1, and *Nobody* by Keith Sweat came with us everywhere we went. He thought this out. He was prepared. And I was weary.

That night he asked me 15 times to have sex with him. I remember praying, *"Jesus, You know I don't want to do this...but I'll lose him if I don't! Could You ever forgive me if I do what he asks? If I promise to marry him?? What's the difference if we do it now or later, so long as we marry?"*

After feeling like I made things as right with Jesus as I possibly could, I consented to my boyfriend's request. We had only been in a relationship for about three weeks, but it felt like an eternity because of the relentless pressure. I lost my virginity that night, and with it, my personal autonomy. I was one with this 21-year-old man. And he cunningly had my full trust. I couldn't help but to blindly trust him now–I had given him absolutely everything.

He dropped me off at my house. I crept back inside, locked the door behind me, quietly made my way to my room, and slipped into the safety of my own bed. There was no conversation with God when I returned that night, only what seemed to be deafening silence. I was forever changed, and I was certain He didn't want to talk to me anymore. I would have grieved the loss immediately, but for the numbness.

I don't ever remember deciding to be numb, and yet, somehow, I was. I quickly cut off thoughts that made me anxious and afraid, assuring myself it would all be okay. I told myself that everything would work out. *It had to work out.* I had nothing left to give. If things didn't go well with my boyfriend, I would only be *damaged goods* to everyone else. There was no place in the church for mistakes like this. *For people like me.* It had to work. I would make certain I was a good girlfriend so he wouldn't leave me.

Whew. I'm gonna need to take my own advice and step away for a bit after writing this chapter. It took a lot out of me. I'm going to go sit in the presence of the Lord, play a card game with my youngest, and fill back up.

This is your tender invitation to do likewise, if you need it.

PART 4

PROCESS WHO GOD IS

CHAPTER 8

CHARACTER OF GOD

What about the times in your story that left you feeling alone and helpless? Do you know with certainty that God is good in those very moments? What about His attribute of tenderness–do you feel His tender pursuit of you at the deepest levels of your being?

"Why does all this even matter?" you may be asking. It matters because *if who He is hasn't yet transcended your reality*, you cannot possibly walk in His freedom and redemptive power. The enemy is using your own story against you to keep you silent and enslaved. There are questions you may not even know your soul is desperately seeking the answers to–and that's where fear, doubt, anger, and foolishness reside.

I am devoting this chapter to the evidence of how He reveals Himself to me in the day-to-day, endearing my heart to His anew. This chapter is for the skeptic.

Do you ever hear someone talking about God and it just feels fake? Have you found yourself responding with sound Christian rhetoric when someone asks, "How are you doing?" but you feel utterly detached from the truth of your response? Being skeptical means that you doubt something is true or useful.

Past trauma, church hurt, betrayal of trust, or never having someone you could rely on all fuel our inner skeptic. Someone who was supposed to care for you took advantage of your vulnerability for their own personal gain. You were exploited to satisfy someone's fleshly lusts or their greed for power, control, or money. When you were desperate and alone, no one came to your defense or offered you needed respite. I'm willing to bet you don't have to search your memory bank very hard to find a place where your faith feels thin–or even non-existent.

Whether we realize it or not, we transpose these feelings onto God. *Why didn't You step in? Why didn't You send someone? Why didn't You act? Do You even care?* Now, if you've been raised in a theologically sound church, you may not even allow these thoughts to surface. Hear me, sound theology is GOOD. We need to first know so we can then believe. But when we stop at the knowing and use it to make ourselves feel more put together than others–or use our knowledge to make others feel less so we can divert attention from that pet sin in the closet–then even theology becomes just another tool in the enemy's tool box.

Yes, Satan uses even *good things* to distract, destruct, and divide believers all day, every day.

Taking a look at the fruit we are producing can help us determine if our inner skeptic is roaming wild and free, keeping us numb to and unconcerned with the real work of God in our midst.

Why even share my story here in this book? It's heavy to read, I know. It's even heavier to write. The reason I alternate between my story and lessons God has taught me is because what I write must come from a place of utter dependence. It must be real or it won't reach into *your* brokenness. It is through remaining close to the work He has done in the midst of what nearly undid me as a human being that His heart transcends my writing. Through my own redemption story, I get a handle on the gospel anew. Through the very things I felt for so long disqualified me as a pastor's wife, His truth is made tangible.

Apart from Him, I have nothing to offer. So I lay down my Bible college answers, and what I think befits a pastor's wife, and instead invite you into a real space of His work and grace.

God's goodness is chasing me down in the day-to-day, and it's chasing you down too. You may know in your mind who He is–His attributes and character might be something you've heard about since childhood–but mere head knowledge doesn't hold the power to transform. Or, maybe you're unsure of who God actually is, but you've been watching from afar and are now leaning in to understand Him. Allowing who He is to transcend the deepest places of your heart and soul is where healing is found and hope is anchored to a God who cannot fail and does not abandon His own.

Is being skeptical always bad? Absolutely not. There have been times in my adult life when I or my family have been abused, mistreated, and taken advantage of. Unfortunately, a lot of this has taken place in the church. The church is full of sinners, just like every other place where humans gather. But when there is a masked enemy parading the name of Jesus while causing a tsunami of destruction, it leaves the wounded in utter despair and skeptical of whether or not they can ever trust a church again.

For Chris and I, Jesus has used church hurt to secure in our hearts and minds that He is truly the only One worth our trust and worship. Sometimes we elevate church leadership or methodologies to such a degree that they become idols in our lives. Because we serve a good God who is jealous for us, He can use hurt within the church body to loosen our grip on people or things that aren't safe foundations. People or things that fall apart are, in a way, a gift. They remind us that nothing and no one but God is worthy of our devotion. If something falls apart in front of you, it's an opportunity to surrender it to Jesus. If He sees it as useful for your good and for His glory, He will resurrect it. If not, He will move you into something you never would have stepped into had the previous thing not failed.

I've learned that skepticism, when beneficial, keeps us from believing something just because we hear or see it. While sometimes birthed in pain, skepticism can make us content to wait on God for the next step instead of rushing to esteem someone or something else as our source of hope.

But *skepticism works against us* when it isolates us, pulling us away from God and others out of fear of being hurt again. What God uses to bring us back to His heart, the enemy uses to enslave us to a false security, often in the name of self-preservation.

When I asked Chris his thoughts on this topic, he brought up some more great food for thought. He says to consider the source of your skepticism. Is it rooted in what God has taught you through His Word and your life experiences? When something you thought was healthy is actually unhealthy, it can leave you skeptical. But skepticism can also lead you to trusting in God instead of in man–which isn't a bad thing at all.

This doesn't mean we should never trust people, but that our trust should be placed in God first and foremost. The Bible doesn't say in Proverbs 3:5, "trust in man with all your heart," it says, *"trust in the Lord with all your heart."* (I told you I married a good one…*thank You, Jesus!*)

I don't trust Christianity just because it's emotionally satisfying. Everybody bases their lives on deep convictions that can't be fully proven. There isn't even a lot of agreement on what "proof" actually means. (Although countless prophecies fulfilled throughout the ages definitely bring a validation to Christianity that no other faith can claim.) I trust the God of Christianity because He has proven Himself to me in every aspect of my life. *It's personal proof.* It's Him meeting me in ways no one could possibly know I needed. He has proven enough in both the lack and the plenty, in the trauma and the healing. This is my testimony.

If boldly sharing my testimony leads others to know the God of the Bible and surrender their lives to Him, then that's the power of God at work through me. I refuse to twist arms and force others into my worldview. There's no merit, no rewards, no eternal value in convincing someone of my beliefs for the sake of convincing them. I can say this from personal experience.

Missionary-dating was the only way I thought I'd ever find a boyfriend or husband in my teenage years. Time and time again, any efforts I made to bring a boy over to my way of thinking failed and resulted in much heartache and pain. Finally, I surrendered, telling God I wasn't going to pursue anybody ever again! If He had someone for me, He was going to have to drop him in my lap. And He did.

Neither Chris nor I were looking to date. We became friends in a season of deep personal hurt for us both, but through separate circumstances. Jesus made it clear we were to pursue one another. We were both apprehensive, so we asked friends to help us see potential blind spots and speak into our relationship. God kept making things clear and granting peace each step of the way until we were married in 2004.

Twenty years later, God continues to bless our relationship as we walk surrendered to Him. I often tell Chris that he is never more attractive to me than when he is living fully for Jesus. This isn't something I could've manipulated in his life. It's his own genuine faith journey that I love and am continually blessed by. The way God uses my husband's gifts in my life and the lives of our children endears me anew to Jesus' provision, sacrificial love, and counsel. I couldn't have possibly orchestrated this on my own. My plans were nowhere near as fulfilling. God's work in the lives of human beings is always personal and intimate.

I want to paint a picture for you of just how personal and intimate God is in my own life.

These days I wake up before my family. The house is still and quiet, and I feel a gentle invitation to spend time with Him. I quietly make my way into the bathroom to get ready for the day, then downstairs to start my electric kettle for a fresh pot of pour-over coffee. I like my beans ground freshly before brewing, so I measure three scoops of my current favorite roast and head to the garage to hit "start" on the grinder. This way, I don't wake my family or any Airbnb guests in the suite below. Once the coffee is off to a good start, I head over to the counter to do a final stretch and shaping of my sourdough loaf. It's been bulk-fermenting overnight, and after proofing for 45 minutes, it'll be ready to bake. The goal is to have it coming out of the oven just before I wake the kids. I imagine the smell of fresh bread greets my family just as warmly as it does me. It seems a tangible way of demonstrating my love for my family each day. *Grace.*

I make the froth for my homemade cappuccino with just pure maple syrup and almond milk. I layer it all into my insulated mug and head to the couch where my favorite blanket awaits me. It was hand-crocheted by one of our Airbnb guests and was such a loving and thoughtful gift. As I pull it over my lap, I take a sip of warm coffee and grab my Bible. There was a long season when I would spend time with Jesus only if and when I found a moment throughout my day, but this dedicated time each morning has been so fruitful and life-giving. Feeling perfectly known and loved is the best way I can think of to start my day. *Grace.*

He meets me in the initial reading, whether in Psalms, Galatians, or Isaiah, then tenderly leads me back to certain words or verses. As I lean in to know His heart for me, I am never disappointed. I'm in awe at how He knows just what to say to bring my inner longings and struggles to light in a way that grants perspective and lifts my burdens. I pull out the laptop to write , and with a renewed mind, I have much to share. My weakness for His strength. My shame for His glory. My suffering for His purpose. I give it all up to Him with each word I type, an offering of praise to use as He desires. *Grace.*

Two hours fly by, and the smell of fresh sourdough fills the house. My coffee is cold but nearly gone. Chris has grabbed some sourdough from the morning before, along with the coffee I poured into a thermos for him, gives me a kiss, and heads out the door for the church office. He's been so supportive of my healing journey. Every single aspect of it. I am so very blessed that we get to do this journey together. I wrap up my thoughts, save my work, and head upstairs to wake the kids. We have a slow morning ahead of us, and we all are happy for the intentional pace that makes room for however we may be feeling. Jesus is ready to meet us in it all, I am certain of it. *Please keep my heart connected to Yours so it's You I pour into them today, Lord. They need You more than anything else I could possibly give them. Grace.*

The laundry had piled up next to the couch–about 4 loads worth. It was clean, but it needed folding. I know my kids and I would benefit from sticking with our rhythm of doing school after breakfast, so I begin to read the lesson, even though the mess beside me threatens my sanity. Out of the corner of my eye, I see my youngest begin to fold the laundry. You guys, THIS is Jesus. She hates folding laundry. Like, cries whenever she has laundry to fold. I usually end up folding it with her because I know that the executive function of her sweet brain isn't flourishing. She's a lover and a dancer. A cart-wheeler and a singer. But not a laundry folder. Yet here she is, leaning into this dreaded chore because she knows it would bless her Mama's heart. She folds the entire pile with the sweetest disposition, saying, "It's calming me." *Grace.*

First thing in the morning, we discover our air conditioner has stopped working, and the forecast is 80° for today. As the afternoon rolls around, I know the kids would benefit from a dip in our neighbor's pool to help stay cool. Ya'll, we have been granted access to a beautiful pool right next door, one we don't have to do a thing to maintain. It feels like a hug from Jesus, over and over again. We pack our lunches and head over. I wait for my Instagram post to upload, then I sit for a brief moment and think, "I should be writing my book right now instead of sitting here. And the garden needs my attention–the deer got into the strawberries last night. I don't have time to sit here right now." Then a quiet voice reminds me that I could simply pull out my phone and research "grace." Sitting by the poolside doing research for my book feels a lot better than being stuck in a warm house without air conditioning. *Grace.*

When it's obvious we're nearing that point of just enough time in the pool, but not long enough for meltdowns, I call the kids out and we head back to our house. Chris meets us outside with tools in hand, making his way around to the air conditioning units. He had been to lunch with a small group friend who gave him a solid vote of confidence that Chris could probably fix the air conditioning unit himself. It would literally save us hundreds of dollars. So, my brave husband did some research and is out here trying to tackle it. My heart is instantly grateful for the many ways Chris works hard to provide for our family and save us from unnecessary expenses. (Oh, and yes–he did fix our air conditioner with a $13 part and five minutes of work!) *Grace.*

As I stand there, grateful, the half-eaten strawberry plants catch my eye. At the same time, Jesus heads off my anxiety about the situation with the reminder of the Liquid Fence spray I have in the garage from last year. It's supposedly fox urine, so natural-ish, and actually works great to keep the deer at bay (not the racoons so much!). I grabbed the bottle and sprayed down the strawberries and the hostas. Well, the stubs of the hostas, anyway. Darn deer. Not winning any HOA yard of the month awards. Humility…and *grace.*

After an easy dinner, Daddy plays baseball in the cul-de-sac with the kids while I put another loaf of sourdough into the oven for a sweet friend. I make some tea and play a card game with my youngest. It's been a full day, and the whole family is tired. Bedtime feels necessary. We worked hard for it. I read a bedtime story, and we hug and kiss all our kiddos. It's not perfect, but goodness, our hearts are full. We *get to* do life together each day. *Grace.*

The way He infuses grace into my days…it draws me in and keeps me coming back for more. I am dependent on Him to show up and meet our needs. Just being in His presence soothes my soul and changes my everything.

The next middle-of-the-night pick-up was my boyfriend and his cousin. The time after that, it was his cousin and a boy I had grown up with in school. *What in the world is he doing here in the middle of the night? And why is my boyfriend so busy that he can't come pick me up himself? Now the whole world will know what we're doing. This is awkward and embarrassing. Also, I don't feel very loved by him.*

Each time, I was taken to a different location. It was all so disorienting. But my boyfriend was always there, reassuring me, acting as if it was all normal. He was trying to change my understanding of *normal.* And I trusted him blindly, because I loved him, after all.

After only a couple of weeks, he told me he was being paroled back to California, but he'd be back for me when I was 16. *Just like that? How do you not have control over leaving, but somehow have control over when you'll come back??* It seemed off, but I didn't have the energy to focus on the inconsistencies in his story. He was leaving me. And as much as I wanted to believe that he would indeed come back to marry me someday, the harsh reality was settling in: I didn't actually know if he would come back for me. In all realness, I had a sinking feeling that he never would.

Days and weeks went by with no word from him. My depression weighed so heavily I could hardly bear it. I felt alone and worthless, with no one to console me. To heighten my grief, rumor had it that an upperclassman at school wanted to beat me up. "(William) was her boyfriend too," a friend told me. "Turns out he was picking her up just before or after he was with you." And as if it couldn't get any worse, she was pregnant with his baby.

A few days later, Uncle Mikey reached out to me through a message on my beeper. I called him on the landline, careful to make sure no one was close enough to be suspicious and pick up the other phone in our house. "I'm sorry for what my nephew did to you," he said. "I'm here if you ever need to talk." *For what your nephew did to me?* I thought. *I didn't think it was his decision to leave??* But my reasoning mind stopped there. I was desperate for someone to talk to–someone who knew what I had done but wouldn't condemn me for it. I couldn't take the verbal and emotional beatings. I was too hurt, too broken.

I needed someone who would be gentle with my fragility, someone who didn't need me to explain what I had been through. Uncle Mikey knew. He had been somewhat of a father figure to me the few times I was around him. He looked out for me. So, I decided to take him up on his gentle offer to listen, and I began looking for the next opportunity to talk with him.

CHAPTER 9

IS HE ABSENT

Our first born was only two years old when he began having regular night terrors. I could tell by his cry piercing through the darkness that he was scared, so I quickly ran to hold and comfort him. His tiny little voice quivered as he recounted his dream as best as his little toddler self could. The details were vague, but the fear was real, and it consumed him. He pleaded with me not to leave his side. I stayed with him and comforted him the best way I knew how. "Pray to Jesus, He will always keep you safe," I said, though my voice faded in uncertainty.

Safe? But Jesus didn't keep me safe.

That familiar fear crept in like a thief, stealing my peace there at my son's bedside. The fact was, I didn't know how to lay a foundation of faith for my precious boy that would see him through whatever heartache and pain lay ahead. And it broke me. What rose to the surface was a question I never even knew existed deep within me, where trauma had left its mark:

Where were You in my darkest moments, God?
Where were You when I was being raped?

I wrestled with this for months. In God's sovereignty, we had a church conference that fall, and a biblical soul care pastor–who was a mentor to Chris as he pursued his master's in counseling–was teaching a session on counseling one another with the Word of God within the church. The session was impactful, with so many tangible takeaways we were eager to apply. But I knew I needed just a moment with Pastor Garrett Higbee.

There was a line forming to talk with him after the session. I knew I wouldn't have much time, but Pastor Garrett had a unique gift for making the complicated simple and pointing others to a truth that anchors, so I waited patiently for my turn to speak with him.

Recognizing that many were standing within earshot of our conversation, I leaned into the courage found in the Holy Spirit's prompting and invited him in. "I went to Bible college and am now a pastor's wife, but I need answers to my child's fear that will not fail him later in life. I realize it's because I don't actually know *where God was* in my own moments of trauma, or how He viewed me in the midst of darkness."

He looked at me with so much compassion that I felt Jesus drawing near in that very moment. Gently, he said, "I have had many counselees over the years who have also struggled to know where God was and what His posture was in their moments of trauma. If we were in a counseling setting, and you were here with your advocate (a spouse, friend…someone who is committing to walk alongside you in your healing journey), I would ask a fellow staff member to come in and play the part of Jesus for this session. I would then ask you to physically position Jesus just as you imagine Him when you think back to those dark moments.

"When I have done this with other counselees they always position Jesus far away in the corner of the room, with His back turned towards them. Some even place Him outside of the room, unacquainted with the suffering happening inside. I then ask the *advocate* to position Jesus as He actually was during those moments. Without prompting, the advocate would take Jesus and bring Him near to the victim, oftentimes embracing him or her. Other times, the victim would be placed in Jesus' lap, with His arms wrapped around him or her. Every single time I have done this there isn't a dry eye in the room.

You go back and you tell your baby when he is having night terrors that *Jesus is right there with him*. That He will never leave him nor abandon him in his time of need. The fact is, Jesus was *grieving* when you were being raped. He wasn't angry, nor did He turn His back on you. He was broken for you, and He never once left your side."

Everything changed. Crippling fear gave way to abundant peace and so much healing. Jesus never left me. He was always there. His presence in the midst of our suffering means that we have *an Advocate there in the battle* with us. Had I known this when I was a teenager, it would have surely changed how I responded to the trauma. But, praise Jesus, He made the brain in such an amazing way that it can *heal and relearn* how to respond to the memory of the trauma.

So, how does this change my response to the struggles and warfare I face today? When threatened, I now *run* into Jesus' loving arms, knowing that He is indeed my refuge and strength. Until He returns or calls me home, there will be battles too great for me to face on my own. But I was never created to face them on my own. There is a place I can retreat to, where the enemy cannot touch me–that place is the presence of my Savior, my Advocate, my Redeemer, my God.

Up until this crucial revelation of who Jesus was in my suffering, I had subconsciously decided to robe myself in man-made righteousness–and I did it well. I told you I had grown up in the church, and I knew the part. I fooled myself into thinking that appearing every bit of a pastor's wife was a *proper response* to my brokenness. *Hide it away. Act as if it never happened.* But Jesus, as He does, didn't stop pursuing my heart. He wants the whole thing. I certainly wasn't fooling Him. By only concerning myself with *looking the part* of a pastor's wife, I merely pointed others to myself. I was in a self-made prison and never questioned it–until I was in a space that was safe for me to do so.

Have you asked Jesus, "Where were You in my darkest moments?" I am creating space for you to ask this question right here, right now. *You are safe in this moment.* And He has so much to reveal to you. Friend, my heart's desire for you is to find refuge in the God who never leaves you. Take a moment to let the following verses wash over you as you reflect on how He has been intimately present in your own life.

"You are a hiding place for me; You preserve me from trouble; You surround me with shouts of deliverance." –Psalm 32:7

"I waited patiently for the Lord; He inclined to me and heard my cry. He drew me up from the pit of destruction, out of the miry bog, and set my feet upon a rock, making my steps secure. He put a new song in my mouth, a song of praise to our God. Many will see and fear, and put their trust in the Lord." –Psalm 40:1-3

"Deliver me from sinking in the mire; let me be delivered from my enemies and from the deep waters. Let not the flood sweep over me, or the deep swallow me up, or the pit close its mouth over me. Answer me, O Lord, for Your steadfast love is good; according to Your abundant mercy, turn to me. Hide not Your face from your servant, for I am in distress; make haste to answer me. Draw near to my soul, redeem me; ransom me because of my enemies!" –Psalm 69:14-18

"Behold, God is my salvation; I will trust, and will not be afraid; for the Lord God is my strength and my song, and He has become my salvation." –Isaiah 12:2

"When you go through deep waters, I will be with you. When you go through rivers of difficulty, you will not drown. When you walk through the fire of oppression, you will not be burned up; the flames will not consume you." –Isaiah 43:2 NLT

Can you recall a time when someone came alongside you in such a way that your burden immediately felt lighter? I can recount numerous times when someone has reached out with a question to gain understanding instead of leading with a word of harsh criticism. Some have brought my family a meal in a weary season, sent an unexpected note of encouragement, or simply been *present with me* when I struggled to know God's way through difficulty. These individuals are proof that Jesus is near and never abandons me in my time of need. They have been the tangible handles I have needed to keep my trust anchored in the One who cannot fail me. *God sent them.*

From His heart, He moved these individuals to respond–even at times when I didn't know how to ask for help. And these people made the choice to respond. To inconvenience their day or week to show up and *bear up under* my burden with me. They were under no obligation, yet they leaned into the opportunity the Holy Spirit set before them to embody His heart for His people. I cannot deny the supernatural power behind such a presence. It has kept me putting one foot in front of the other, moving toward Him instead of becoming stagnant and lifeless.

At 42 years of age, Jesus has lovingly brought into my life an astounding number of people who continue to reach out from time to time and spur me on in my faith journey. It's a blessing every single time. But who are the people who are consistently my *people*?

As I mentioned, we began ministry serving teens through youth ministry. It was a beautifully fruitful season, applying what we learned in Bible college to cultivate genuine community. Through this time, our hearts grew for the church at large. Everyone needed community that transcended their current reality–not just Sunday church folk, but people who *live out* what we say we are all about. This kind of living radically defies the culture we find ourselves in and *extends an invitation* to all who are hurting, broken, and searching for tangible evidence to hope.

Then God led us into a season of cultivating this authentic community on a church-wide scale. We call this community *small group*. You may know it as life group, groups, or missional community–or you may have never even heard of the concept.

But what's so special about it? And what does it have to do with knowing how God is present in my suffering?

I have asked several individuals we've done life and community with over the years to share the tangible ways Jesus has proven He is present in our everyday life, namely through their small group. I pray you are as blessed and compelled to lean in as I am through their responses…

"God has revealed through small group that I am not the only person who has experienced church hurt. God has truly shown me His presence by giving me the mental strength to start the process of healing from past trauma. I look at all the bravery God has given each person who has shared their God-story… so glad to be a part of small group. I didn't understand that my story can have a great impact on someone else's life. People are changed by looking at how God has truly shown up in your life. You can preach Scripture to folks all day but if they can't hear what God has done for you and where He has brought you from, then sometimes the Scripture doesn't matter.

"The enemy has lied to me for many years. He told me to leave the past behind and move forward with my life. I can truly see how the past has molded my life…I no longer want to be controlled by triggers but instead be able to manage any trigger that comes up. Now I know that there are Christians who deal with real life issues. If it had not been for small group and experiencing people sharing very vulnerable past and present experiences I would still be leaving the past in the past, which would be a shame.

"I don't know if anyone has ever heard this saying, 'What goes on in this house stays in this house.' This is what I heard as a child, mostly by black people. This is why generation after generation continues to suffer in silence. I said all that to say, God has given me the physical strength to open up and share, and continues to give me the emotional strength of accepting what I've actually lived through."

–Kevina R.

"I think the biggest thing for me is that Jesus' presence is so known and felt amongst our small group that I crave, desire, and am excited for 6:30pm every Monday despite my everyday craziness. Mondays especially are my busiest, most stressful work day of the week. It would be easy for me to not go to group because of the 30-minute drive, being tired from my 9-5, homework, making dinner, and the list goes on...but never once have I felt like not going to group because I know I can come feeling empty and I'll leave full because that's how Jesus intended community and fellowship + His presence."

–Maddy M.

"Small Groups are a place to connect with others and learn more about God. It is a place to be supported in our brokenness, which we don't always like to admit, but we all have. It is a place to be encouraged in just everyday life. Hopefully, it is a place that God uses to help direct our next steps towards obedience to Him. As a leader, small groups can be messy with everyone's expectations and personalities. But if we

never step out of our comfort zone, we wouldn't need a Comforter!! It is definitely worth it."

–Aaron K.

"Small Group has reminded me that Jesus wants us to be in community, and He will work through other believers to help us understand things we struggled with when working through them on our own. Having a group of believers around you also helps me remember every saint has a past and every sinner has a future, not any credit to works, but because of Christ's sacrifice. That said, I feel it has also helped me see myself how Christ does when I otherwise would just be my own biggest critic."

–Matt B.

"I know that Jesus is present in the midst of everyday life through small group when I read and hear our group reach out on our chat throughout the week to share their struggles and trials/praise reports and how we respond with encouragement and prayers. It keeps us connected to each other. I see Jesus working in lives as we live out His Word when it says to confess our faults one to another and to pray for each other. That allows us to be vulnerable and show His love and compassion for our brothers and sisters."

–Varonaki P.

"Before I was part of a small group, I was not spending time with the Lord and/or reading my Bible every day. However, when we would get together with our small group I saw how I benefited from hearing how God

had taught, encouraged, or convicted others during their daily times with Him. I found myself wanting that for myself and began making it the priority that I knew it should have been in my life.

It helped me become EXCITED to spend time with the Lord as He would use what I had learned to bless others in our small group by what I had read or prayed for that week. And that turned into a habit that has truly become my daily bread! Not only that, but it has shown us how we must teach these things to our children and now seeing the fruit of God's work in their quiet times with Him has been one of the best parts of parenting.

Another way that small group changed my life was learning what it means to BE the church in a way that exemplifies the early church found in Acts where the believers shared all that they had with one another. Our small groups have helped people move, have held garage sales to raise money for missions trips, have done service projects together in the community, watched each other's children, brought dinners over for new babies, times of grief, or when overwhelmed by life, have taken trips to the emergency room together, have raised money for adoption, have sat with each other in silence in times of need, have confronted each other gently in times when truth was missing, have served in tandem at church in various ministries, have been there to celebrate birthdays and promotions, and holidays when family was not nearby, and we have also prayed together over life's most tender of needs. In essence the small groups we have been part of have operated like a family. We did not pick and choose who was in our groups, but we can see how God brought us all together with our own individual gifts that He bestows to us all to grow up into Christ alongside each other!"

–Renae C.

"This past year, I've felt the presence of the Lord through...receiving/sending voice memos to one another...We use these to share all that God is doing in our lives, to pray over one another, or even to share some hardships that we're walking through...It just shows me that God can show up through anything, at any time, you just have to be willing and expectant."

–Jill K.

"We have really grown in friendship...we all want to have people hold us accountable. We have a group chat of just the guys that we send what we read in the Word each day...We all have been more consistent in our time in the Word because of this."

–Michael K.

"When I think of small groups and God showing up I think about two things. In the tangible things like providing support for each other whether that is a meal after a birth of a child or a replaced knee. Or getting together to help with moving or a yard project or cleaning up something for someone. Small group is being the hands and feet and meeting real needs for the people around us. Another thing I think about

is just space. Space to process, space to feel, space to confess our sin and space to share in the blessings that God is giving. There aren't a lot of times that people are able to just sit and ask questions or talk about themselves and how God is at work but having that time and space to think and reflect is something beautiful. To do it amongst other believers who are happy for you or will encourage you when you are feeling weak or help navigate through a conflict, THAT is a precious gift that living in community provides and that our good Father gives us. He shows up through His people."

–Leah F.

"We experience the presence of Christ personally and powerfully through our small group. We are family to each other. 'Together' is a key word for our small group family. We pray together and play together. We cry and we laugh. We study the Word of God together, making applications to our lives and holding each other accountable. We have prayed for one another's children all through the years and now pray as these 'kids' are young adults. We pep-talk each other through the trials of parenting as well as the issues of caring for and saying goodbye to aging parents. We cry together and hold each other at funerals and dance together at weddings. We vacation together and the guys golf many fundraising events each year. We attend trivia nights for St Jude's and mission trips and serve together in our community. Need I say more? Oh yes, we eat together... a lot!

To sum up, we: study, pray, cry, laugh, play, celebrate, commiserate, serve, love & eat...together!"

–Darlene T.

Did you catch it in their testimonies? *Jesus is always present.* He never leaves you nor forsakes you. And He proves it in the memory of past hurt and trauma, and in the present through His people and His creation.

Will you lean in to know this truth for yourself? What opportunities has He laid in front of you to do life with your brothers and sisters in Christ? How can you embody His presence in the life of another? Is there someone specific He is laying on your heart now?

This is a safe space...but may it also be a *sacred space* as you know Him more intimately. Please respond according to how He is tenderly leading you into more than you could possibly know on your own, and then be expectant for Him to show up in ways that change your everything.

As I shared, I was in N.J.R.O.T.C. throughout my high school years. I had many friends in the program and really enjoyed my time with them. We did so many activities together outside of school hours. I was captain of the unarmed drill team and a member of the orienteering team, which involved using a compass and a map to search the desert for miles, with the intent to locate all the markers and be the first team back to the base. It was grueling, but it bonded us.

In my freshman year of high school, I was really trying to find my way and wanted everyone to believe I was strong. Like, abnormally strong. I aimed to be the first female Navy SEAL, although the thought actually terrified me. I had no idea what it would require, but I was desperate to maintain a tough exterior and rise to any challenge that faced me. My peers cheered me on, and I was well-supported amongst my N.J.R.O.T.C. family. It was the most consistent safe space I had throughout those four years of high school. No one comes to mind who could relate with my Christian faith, but they were also okay with me being a Christian. For a public-school setting, it was a pretty special community.

It was our first annual lock-in, and we were all looking forward to it. For some crazy reason, staying up all night is highly appealing to high-schoolers. Especially when friends, food, and unlimited soda were involved. That Friday came, and news went out to the students that the lock-in had been canceled, and we were to tell our parents. I knew this would perhaps be my only opportunity to talk with Uncle Mikey, so I called a friend from NJROTC and asked if he could pick me up and drop me off at a friend's house. He agreed, but I told him not to mention the cancellation of the lock-in to my parents. As we pulled up to the apartment complex, my friend's eyes grew wide with concern. "I don't feel right about dropping you off here, Crystal. It doesn't seem like a safe place," he said. I assured him (and myself) that it was okay because I knew Uncle Mikey, and he would look out for me. I got out of the car and watched as my friend reluctantly pulled away. This was long before the days of cell phones, so as he left the deteriorated parking lot, I truly was without a lifeline.

I walked into the now-familiar apartment where Uncle Mikey was waiting for me. He was the only one there at first, but he seemed distant as he handed me a 40oz of Boone's Strawberry Hill. "Is this all for me?" I asked. "It sure is," he replied. I guess alcohol is how he wanted to help me cope with my grief. Not many words were exchanged before a group of people walked into the apartment. My anxiety went through the roof when I saw a fellow-highschooler named Robert walk through the door. He and I had a run-in a couple of months before this–I confronted him in a letter about his arrogance and pride after he pressured me to have sex with him while hanging out somewhere I shouldn't have been. Mutual friends told me it was a brave move, as he was known for beating his girlfriend. Since writing the letter, I had only seen him on school grounds, where I felt protected.

"*I don't feel like you're safe here…*we should go," Uncle Mikey whispered in my ear. I didn't even hesitate as the fear of what Robert could do to me had me frozen. So I got up and walked out with Uncle Mikey.

A man I didn't recognize walked out with us. He was in his late twenties and never said a word to me, but he and Uncle Mikey spoke discreetly back and forth as we left the apartment complex.

I had no idea where we were heading, but it felt good to put some distance between us and the known danger. As we walked down Apache Trail, a main road in our town, there was an older teen girl standing there in the middle of the sidewalk. *Perhaps she was waiting for the city bus?* I paid her little attention until the guy walking with us began talking with her. We stopped and waited for them. There was some back and forth–none of which was audible to me. Uncle Mikey was noticeably uneasy. He made no eye contact with me nor did he say much. He was fidgety. I guess I didn't really know him well enough to think it was strange, even still, it felt off to me at the time. Before I could dwell on his odd behavior, we were walking again–this time with the girl.

We arrived at an old, Western-themed hotel. My family and I had passed it a billion times as we ran errands and went to The Feedbag, a local restaurant with good biscuits and gravy. I had never been inside this hotel, though. Uncle Mikey walked up to the front desk where a couple of teenage girls stood behind the counter. While he gave his check-in information to one of the young clerks, the other stood and stared intently at our group of four. She couldn't look away. Her gaze met mine, and I immediately felt ashamed as she looked me up and down.

This is not what you're thinking...gross! These men are old enough to be my dad!

I hadn't even considered how things appeared until that moment, but I quickly dismissed it. I knew why I was there–*I needed someone to talk to* about the mess I found myself in. I needed comfort and reassurance that everything would be okay. I needed protection from someone hurting my heart again. *These* were the only reasons I stood in the lobby of a hotel with people I hardly knew–because Uncle Mikey had offered to "talk about it" when I called him a couple of weeks earlier. And I was too hurt to comprehend any other reality.

But what if this critical glance from the young girl behind the counter was yet another warning flag from God? Why had I dismissed it so quickly? The truth was, I was 14 years old and had never grappled with the depths of evil lurking in the darkness. But what if I had allowed myself to feel what this young hotel clerk was obviously thinking? Would it have changed the trauma that took place just moments later?

Discernment wasn't a skill I had developed at this point in my life. My parents had kept me safe from evil people simply by enforcing rules. Perhaps my developing brain couldn't grasp such hard realities. Maybe my parents were unaware of how evil would prey on me while at a slumber party in a room full of girls on my volleyball team.

What made *me* a vulnerable target? How can I, as a mom of three, prepare my precious children *should evil find them* in places where *they should be safe*?

The landscape has changed since I was 14 years old. Predators don't need to meet our children face-to-face to groom them. The internet offers more opportunities for evil people to find victims than we, as parents, can keep up with. But you know what, Mom and Dad? We were created for such a time as this. We can learn new things, and we can make time to ensure our kids stay safe.

In the Appendix, I've gleaned some practical tips from a local ministry that will help us, as parents, be proactive in keeping our kids safe from today's threats.

Jesus is leading Chris and me to make space to cultivate our relationship with our children, which is a crucial step in making them difficult targets. But of course, nothing is a guarantee. Trust in Jesus must be our resting place. As they get older, our children are trying to figure out who they are and how to connect with the world around them.

Predators are looking for vulnerabilities they can exploit, grooming your child for their own evil pleasure and gain. I'm going to say this gently because I am reminding myself as well: being too busy isn't an excuse to avoid the hard and beautiful work of creating a safe space for our kids to be seen, known, and loved. If you are too busy, too scared, or too hurt to be who your kids need you to be, you can be certain someone else *will* make time for them. Lean into the *grace* that is found in your current reality, and ask Jesus to show you what it looks like to make space for what matters in these years.

A few words of encouragement before closing out this chapter…*parents, you were created for this*. It's true. Jesus knew all about the things that would hold you back from connecting on a heart level with your children, and He still chose you to be their Mom or Dad. The life-giving truth that changes everything is that when we, as parents, know *who* we are and *whose* we are, we can love our children with Jesus as our perfect portion. He always knows what to do, and when we are walking by His Spirit, He will guide us to be what our kids need us to be as they grow, all the while pointing them to Him as their perfect portion. They won't take the bait from the enemy because they won't be searching for meaning and worth in the wrong places.

It's about being healthy and *being present*, pointing our kids to the only One ever worthy of their trust, affections, and whole hearts. *This is how we get a handle on it*. It is possible. And Jesus knows the way in your unique circumstances. Ask Him what your next step is in cultivating the kind of relationship that makes your child a difficult target as they lean into who He created them to be, and then make some space to listen to His response.

CHAPTER 10

IS HE GRIEVING

Every time I thought back to those dark moments of my abuse, I pictured Jesus shaking His finger at me in disapproval, His back turned towards me, fully rejecting me. I had, after all, lied to my parents about where I was going and who I would be with. (*Can you tell how much mileage the enemy got out of this one little lie?!*) I knew much of God as a righteous judge. He is holy, or *set apart*, and tells us to be set apart too. Every bit of me was desperate to be accepted by Him somehow; I just couldn't see how my scarlet letter fit into the story He was writing. But being entirely wrong about His posture towards me in my most desperate moments made Him seem distant and cold.

"There is therefore now no condemnation for those who are in Christ Jesus. For the law of the Spirit of life has set you free in Christ Jesus from the law of sin and death."
—Romans 8:1-2

Jesus felt emotion. We see it throughout the Bible. He was human in every way, yet still God. The thing is, *Jesus actually invented emotion.* His scope of emotional experience has always far exceeded our own. But up until a decade ago, I saw Jesus as only either pleased with me or displeased. My trauma, among other factors, was limiting the relational dimension I could use with God and others. He was calling me to go deeper that night at my son's bedside. The gripping fear brought on by his night terrors deserved so much more than I could give him. It was a depth I had never explored on my own, and it wrecked me. But as I previously shared, it also forced me to seek answers that would ground his little heart and mind to a peace that could be known not only in the night terrors but also in whatever lay before him in life. This truth sat heavy on my chest...*I couldn't protect my babies from every evil.*

There, in the 2am darkness, I comforted my two-year-old as best as I knew how, while I simultaneously begged God for answers. No, I *demanded* answers. I refused to be numb this time. *My boy needed me to be present* and to find him a truth that could not be shaken, only built upon. God gave me the awareness that these were foundation-building years for him, and so I determined to settle for nothing less than knowing more of who He actually is in our suffering.

In my head, God was worth my trust, but this truth needed to make its way into my past hurts, which had left me exposed and caused me to shut down. If my son hadn't cried out for help, *I may have never cried out for help* in asking the question that lingered inside me for years. I didn't know I was stuffing it down, trying hard to appear healthy to every onlooker. My doubt caused anxiety, and at times I pulled away in subconscious self-preservation mode instead of leaning in. *But my body remembered.* It carried the intensity of the hurt, and when threatened, it shut down peripheral functions so my core could survive. Numbness, dissociation, and distractions–so I wouldn't have to sit in the hard–these were all ways I coped. But Jesus created me to walk in *fullness of life*, to have life abundant. Not apart from hurt, but *through* it. He needed me to intimately understand His posture towards me in my darkest, most fear-filled moments.

"The fact is that Jesus was *grieving* when you were being raped. He wasn't angry, nor did He turn His back on you. He was broken for you, and He never once left your side." The moment Garrett Higbee spoke these words to me after I invited him into my most vulnerable struggle with God, the Holy Spirit testified together with my spirit that it was indeed true. Immediately, peace swept in like a tidal wave of comfort that fortified my wavering trust. I had never before been able to picture Jesus grieving. It was a picture of tenderness in the nearness. He wasn't just *there* with me in those moments–He was *grieving* what was happening to me. He didn't send my boyfriend to rape me because I snuck out of the house. He didn't send Uncle Mikey to rape me because I lost my virginity. *How could I have possibly believed these horrible lies for so many years?!*

Seattle Christian Counseling offers helpful insight on the matter. "A spiritual crisis is created when a person with past trauma experiences a life situation that triggers feelings associated with past hurts. But shutting down receptive parts of the heart to manage overwhelming feelings of trauma comes at a cost. It's like getting a piece of glass stuck in a wound and letting the skin heal over it. Eventually, it needs to be cut out for the person to regain full use of that part of their body. Similarly, a person can only give to others for so long before they collapse, needing someone to take care of them.[1]

In my story, Jesus used this all-too-familiar feeling of crippling fear in my son to stir up a fighter within me. Freezing or running away was my only response to fear up until this point, but now, as a Mama, there was no other option but to *lean in and fight*. Jesus knew exactly what would bring forward movement in my healing, and He oversaw every detail until I saw freedom from the lie that I am alone in my sufferings with a God who is unacquainted with and unbothered by my pain.

"Since then we have a great high priest who has passed through the heavens, Jesus, the Son of God, let us hold fast our confession. For we do not have a high priest who is unable to sympathize with our weaknesses, but one who in every respect has been tempted as we are, yet without sin." —Hebrews 4:14-15

"Even though I walk through the valley of the shadow of death, I will fear no evil, for You are with me; Your rod and your staff, they comfort me." –Psalm 23:4

There were safeguards in place to keep me out of danger as a child. I went outside of those safeguards in my teen years. I put myself in spaces where my parents couldn't protect me. And God allowed it. It's not that He wanted this for me, but He allowed it because He didn't create robots. He created humans, made in His image. In stepping outside of safeguards, I was exercising the free will given to me by my Creator.

But what happens when we have a wrong belief about God? Our decisions will stem from that wrong belief. My craving for acceptance stemmed from my belief that I was not accepted by God unless I was perfect. It felt like an impossible standard–and it was. When a relationship with a boy came my way that made me feel beautiful and accepted, I threw all caution to the wind and jumped in headfirst, without considering the consequences. I was going to will it to work because I was desperate for acceptance. I thought I could control the outcome. My beliefs blinded me, failed me, and left me vulnerable to evil.

Understanding the sovereignty of God's control teaches me how to live with my limits, to accept my limits, and to rest in my limits. It leaves room for grace to do what only grace can do in my life, and then it flows through my life into the lives of others.

Could God have stopped the abuse? *Absolutely, yes.* He could have commanded an army to come to my defense and bring down justice on my abuser without even blinking an eye. I believe with everything in me that He could have. *Then why didn't He?*

By no means will I allow the pages of this book to pass by without addressing this by testifying to His power *through suffering*. Here's the deal: the pastor's wife in me wants desperately to have a polished answer for you. In fact, I have camped out here in this chapter for more than a week–which is a long time considering I have knocked out 13 chapters in 4 weeks already. Jesus just hasn't given me clarity on this for a reason unknown to me. It's frustrating. I want to lean in, know it, and then move on. Gosh, it's hard.

I will continue to lean in to know His heart more deeply on this, but I just feel Him calling me to *surrender* right now. Surrender what I think I need for what God *knows I need.*

Hear me, this is not to say that God has been silent this week as I've wrestled with what He has permitted in my story versus what He has caused in my story. I believe with all my heart that there is a difference, and that it matters profoundly. So, here's *how He has met me this week* as I have intentionally drawn near to Him in the struggle…

*I knew I needed to hear Chris' heart on this. He is discerning and wise with how he applies truth to real life. It's literally a gift of his that has blessed and embraced me and hundreds of others over the years for God's Kingdom work. I loved the evening we had leaning in together on my venture for answers. It grew our bond closer as a husband and wife, and grew my trust in Jesus as He was so tender with me through my husband. Again.

*I have listened to so many podcasts from wise counselors that have compelled me to keep leaning in to know His heart on this. Even though it isn't clear now, He is doing such a mighty work as I wait on Him. I am being changed in the waiting, and I'm not the same person I was just a week ago. I am more fortified and prepared for battle. *I am healing, even as I wait for answers.*

*I have found rest and joy in just being. I've done lots of things this week, but I haven't been searching for my identity in any of them. Jesus has held me secure and keeps bringing me back to His presence–whether I'm doing yard work, visiting with neighbors, maintaining the home, waking up to treat stubborn overnight blood sugar lows, baking, gardening, flipping the Airbnb, serving my family and church family. I feel Him intimately near.

*This morning's message was exactly what I needed. Our senior pastor stood before us and shared that he was struggling with God. He said that he and God are not on good terms right now. *So vulnerable*. I wholly leaned in, expectant for God to show up. My pastor said that he was going to preach from this place of struggle, and encouraged us to invite Jesus into the things we are currently grappling with. "Relinquish your need to forcibly resolve your problems and present your heart to God for resolution," read one of the sermon points. It was as if God was having a one-on-one conversation with me, encouraging me to cease striving for answers in this chapter of my story, and just trust Him to work it out how He knows is best for me. *I hear You, Jesus, and I will choose surrender.*

*Today is Mother's Day and I am reminded anew of just how imperative it is that I continue healing from my past hurts so I can model His heart to my children in these tender, formative years. They base so much of their understanding of who He is on how we parent them. What a beautiful and sobering reality that keeps me desperate for more of Him every single day! The grace in it all is that He can redeem in their lives what Chris and I make messy. Gosh, that's good news! If all we do well is point them to the fact that we aren't perfect and that we *need* our Savior, that's a major win. But I believe Jesus will do exceedingly more than we could ever hope for as parents if we keep offering up our everything for His Kingdom purposes, not withholding a thing but quick to hand over whatever He reveals as deterrents to our relationship with Him and others.

To be sure, God is very present in the waiting. His intentionality goes far beyond mere answers to the questions weighing on our hearts and minds. He hears us, but even when we don't get the answers we demand, He is working through everything in our proximity to capture our hearts. Could it be that He knows the answer isn't the actual biggest need of our souls? Sometimes, I think He just proves He's near and listening, and that His heart is tender toward us as we search for answers to hard things. I believe we will know all the things one day in glory, but until then…finding His presence is more than enough.

We live in a time where we are surrounded by many who have paved the way. They have been doing the heart work in the midst of grief, and in doing so have made space for us to heal in a way that stands together with Jesus in truth. Please allow me to create a safe space for you again here.

You *must* go back to your pain for the purpose of healing, but don't stay there. The fact is that you *do* need to heal in order to walk in the fullness of who God created you to be. When you choose not to go back and feel what you need to feel for the purpose of healing, it costs you greatly. Your actual body is overstressed as it tries to carry the weight of past pain that has yet to be surrendered to God for His purposes and glory. If you don't revisit past pain, it will remain inside you and come out at inopportune times. There is no shortcut to healing.

There is often so much grief in the healing. But it brings me into a right relationship with God to know who He is and who I am. He is a compassionate God who *moves toward brokenness*.

"Rejoice with those who rejoice, weep with those who weep." —Romans 12:15

Me being raped was not God's judgment towards me; it has somehow become the path to my redemption. A path that I find myself taking over and over again when I have lost my way in the midst of either fear or mere religion. Whether or not He made this path for me is unclear at this time. But He is making every bit of it purposeful, even as I write.

I willingly embrace my darkest moments because it is in these most despairing parts of my real-life story that I find the reality of who He is…a good God who has proven worthy of my heart's pursuit. *Not one other thing will satisfy*. I know in the depths of my soul that every other thing actually leads to death. So, as I recall my darkest moments, I choose Jesus again, and again. Pastor Joshua Broome, a former porn-star allowing Jesus to redeem his past, says, "You're only as free as you're willing to be honest." Our freedom is found as we stand with God in the truth about our past and present. Refusing to face the hard parts of our stories only ever enslaves. I choose freedom. And so, I share my story. And you should too.

We made our way into our hotel room. My mind was definitely not engaging with my current reality, but my body was tense. I hoped for the best, combatting my uneasiness about the situation–which honestly felt so off. The room had two queen beds. The couple I still hadn't met sat on the edge of the bed on the farthest side of the room, while Uncle Mikey and I stood by the small set of table and chairs on the other side of the room. I don't remember how or why, but I was smoking cigarettes for the first time in my life. Paired with the wine cooler, I felt physically ill. All I wanted to do was fall asleep to be relieved of the physical sickness and complete uneasiness of the situation I found myself in.

Seconds after Uncle Mikey turned the lights out, the couple in the bed next to us began to have sex. The room was not that big and it was obvious. *What is wrong with people?! Who does this with others in the room?!!* I was disgusted and quite frustrated that somehow the situation had just gotten even more unbearable.

And then, out of nowhere and without warning, Uncle Mikey raped me. My heart and mind were caught up in complete and utter terror. *He's old enough to be my dad! How is this happening?! How do I wake up from this nightmare?!!*

Although in complete shock and still physically impaired by the alcohol and tobacco, somehow I found the strength to tell him *NO. Stop. I don't want to.* Over and over again I repeated myself. But it was as if *I had no voice* because not one person in that small room heeded my cry. The lack of response to my emergency left me mentally and physically unable to do anything other than shut down. My mind attempted to escape the trauma as a last resort. All my energy went to *simply surviving.* I had no plan. There was no one to help me there in that room, even though capable adults were present. I was completely and utterly alone in the darkness with *pure evil.*

This night remained in the darkness for nearly twenty years. My mind wouldn't let me revisit the memory without my body shutting down physically and emotionally. The neural pathways in my brain were broken by the trauma. Over the years, my mind quickly skipped over the memories because I was still trying to survive them. But my body grew tense–*and still does*–when I smell cigarette smoke, enter into a hotel that feels even slightly shady or unkept, feel as though I have no voice when in the presence of evil, when I am emotionally, verbally, spiritually, or mentally abused by those capable of and responsible for leading and protecting me, and when I feel gaslit after bravely stepping into healing and then advocating for my family and others to do the same. These are the triggers that come to mind. And there are more.

By God's grace and strength, I am growing through the very things that would keep me in the dark and without a voice. Because I now know His call on my life, I refuse to be silenced. This work that Jesus is doing–bringing me out of the stifling darkness and into the glorious light–will be given space and utmost importance every day I have breath in me. It must. And because He is empowering me to know His purpose in my story, I advocate for others to know it in the darkest places of their stories too.

Here's the deal with triggers–*they can be redeemed.* When we invite Jesus to reclaim our trauma and past hurt for His purposes and good, He will heal our broken neural pathways and use what the enemy intended for our destruction to make us more sensitive to evil in our midst. We become more attuned than those who haven't experienced such evil or who haven't yet begun their healing journey.

About a year and a half ago, I prayed through my fear, asking Jesus to give me eyes to see those around me who are crying out for help but have been silenced. Then I prayed He would move me toward them as an extension of His heart, that I would not be one who looks away from the suffering and oppressed just because it's hard and messy. Now that I am committed to being brave in Jesus and walking in the light, I have witnessed God open my eyes to see things in plain sight that are somehow hidden from others. It's an evil that lurks and threatens the very peace Jesus created us to walk in. I am learning what it looks like to walk with the Spirit in exposing it for what it is, so it no longer has power.

Of course, He doesn't call us to do this alone. But not everyone is willing to welcome the discomfort that accompanies being brave. For years, I wasn't ready. But now that He's brought me this far in exposing darkness in my own life, I can't stop. There is no going back to numbness or the ignorant belief that, if I don't give it thought, it isn't there. Maybe it looks like continuing to sound the alarm and not growing weary in doing so. It for sure looks like setting up boundaries with unhealthy, sometimes "toxic" people so I can continue walking in the freedom that Jesus has set before me. Evil wants to seek and destroy everything good. It *must not be granted space* in our lives.

Evil exposes itself. It condemns, attacks, silences, chokes out, and vehemently opposes the work of God in your life, leaving confusion, fear, and oppression in its wake. The hardest reality for a professing believer is acknowledging that there are evildoers not just in the world at large, but also in the church body where we worship. Satan himself masquerades as an angel of light.

"And what I am doing I will continue to do, in order to undermine the claim of those who would like to claim that in their boasted mission they work on the same terms as we do. For such men are false apostles, deceitful workmen, disguising themselves as apostles of Christ. And no wonder, for even Satan disguises himself as an angel of light. So it is no surprise if his servants, also, disguise themselves as servants of righteousness. Their end will correspond to their deeds." –2 Corinthians 11:12-15

"We must stop blindly trusting people, even those who claim the name of Jesus, and start being shrewd as snakes while remaining innocent as doves."
–Matthew 10:16-18 NIV

Your posture towards evil doers is crucial. *But what if they're someone close to you? What if they're a family member?* Adam Young, a licensed Christian counselor, has made readily available tools to help you discern who in your life is an ordinary sinner, an evil person, or a wicked person. We must first discern who we are dealing with before we can respond in a way that honors God.

I've heard it said too many times in the church that "we all have sin, so you just need to give them grace," when discussing individuals who have caused harm. Most people will stack hands on the fact that someone who is physically abusive is a threat and they will set up safeguards to protect themselves and their loved ones. But someone who is mentally, emotionally, or spiritually abusive often escapes being openly red-flagged.

Adam Young and any good counselor–including my husband–will caution you that just because someone is a wicked person today doesn't mean they will always be. However, not writing someone off does not mean you permit them to continue hurting you or your loved ones.

On Adam's podcast, *The Place We Find Ourselves*, he explains how to discern what kind of person you are dealing with in a 4-part series called *Engaging With Someone Who Has Harmed You* (episodes 93-96). Is the person willing to ask, "How have I hurt you? How have I done wrong?" If they are willing to listen and hear you, then you're dealing with a *normal everyday sinner*. Simply tell them how they've hurt you. They will listen to you, express sorrow over their wrong, and ask you how they can make it right. They have the willingness to hear they have hurt you and repair the wrong that they have done.

A *wicked person*, however, will not hear you. Instead, they will be quick to find a scapegoat for the wrong they did, often leaving you confused and guilty, even though *they* caused the harm. Gaslighting is a common tactic they use to deflect attention away from their sin instead of taking ownership. They want you to feel as though you are the one in the wrong simply because you shed light on their sin.

The response to those who have harmed you is always love. But here's the deal–*love challenges the status quo*. When you love someone well, the status quo is blown out of the water, and that person's heart will either be softened towards you or hardened because of how well you loved them. Their response to you is not a good measure of whether you've been loving and honoring.

When was the last time you called out someone displaying a pattern of harm? Holding your tongue if you have anything controversial or challenging to say is not how Christ showed us to love others. There is nothing honoring about sweeping things under the rug. *Taking manipulative power away is what Jesus did all the time*. Speaking truth in love is how you fight for more depth, honesty, and intimacy with that person. The big picture goal is reconciliation. Reconciliation, at its core, is overcoming evil with good. You cannot reconcile with a wicked person until they begin putting their wickedness to death. Wicked people have made thousands of decisions over the years to deceive themselves into thinking they are without fault. They believe they haven't hurt you, so, in their eyes, whatever you say is just untrue and you are being too sensitive.

The best gift you can give someone unaware of the cancer within them is to help them feel guilt regarding their sin again by refusing to submit to the status quo that has allowed them to comfortably live as a shell of the person they were created to be. You must walk in freedom while in relationship with them, refusing to submit to a yoke of slavery (Galatians 5:1). Adam Young goes into practical ways to live and communicate with people you love who are wicked in the fourth part of the podcast series. While I don't agree with all of his views, his counsel on this topic and many others is exceptional and has provided Chris and me with so much clarity as we heal and cultivate safe spaces.

Lysa Terkeurst has also written a helpful book on this topic–*Good Boundaries and Goodbyes*–where she leans into her own real-life pain, sharing how Jesus and wise counselors helped her navigate setting up boundaries with those close to her who fell into the camp of being wicked.

The good news is that you were not created to be under the power or control of anyone or anything except a loving, tender God. You do not have to be enslaved because of someone else's sin. One of the hardest things Chris and I have had to do as we heal from past hurt is confront those who have harmed us. It seems easier to just let things be, to avoid challenging the status quo, but what's at stake is not only our loved one's repentance and redemption but also our own health and peace as we succumb to their manipulation and fear tactics.

We were created for more. No more settling for false, superficial peace. Jesus knows true freedom, and He knows how to get us walking in it where we are stuck.

Let's lean in with all we have, utterly surrendering what we once knew in exchange for His way through difficult relationships–where hope is found and the invitation for biblical reconciliation is always open.

When we understand that God's stance in our moments of abuse is one of *grieving*, it helps us navigate our current healing journey. It reveals those who echo His heart–*providing encouragement and clarity*–versus those who echo a spirit of shame, fear, and condemnation–*silencing and enslaving us. It matters* which voices we heed. Setting up healthy boundaries is a must if we are to heal and allow His redemptive work to take center stage in our lives.

CHAPTER 11

IS HE GOOD

Both saved and unsaved alike wrestle with this question: "How can a good God allow such bad things to happen?" Reconciling who He is with the brokenness within and around us can feel utterly impossible. Yet that's exactly the backdrop Jesus does His best work against–the impossible. The stark contrast between brokenness and goodness causes us to call everything we know into question. After years of struggling toward His heart, I believe with everything in me that our good God proves He's good *through broken things.*

"The Lord is good to all; He has compassion on all He has made." –Psalm 145:9 NIV

One of the reasons we get hung up is because we often project our human idea of "goodness" onto God, rather than allowing the Scriptures to define what it means. The God of the Bible is spotlessly good and full of integrity. He cannot do wrong, as it's a violation of His own character. (Psalm 92:15; 1 John 3:2-6)

I didn't question God's goodness during the abuse–at least not in my mind. I was honestly too traumatized to process what I was feeling. I suppressed the memories of what happened with every ounce of willpower I had. Of course, my brain aided in this process, as we have previously discussed. It wasn't until Jesus invited me to surrender my whole story for His redemptive purposes that the question surfaced: *"Are you really good, and if so, why did you allow those things to happen to me?"*

This call to surrender came during the same season that our firstborn was very sick. His illnesses began at three months old with a nasty cold. At six months old, he had croup. At nine months, it was pneumonia. And just about every month after that, his breathing difficulties would surface again–so quickly and severely that he had to be placed on nasty steroids just to take the edge off. We suffered through his first twenty months of life like this, with prescription medications being added one on top of another, none of which did a thing to address the root cause of the inflammation in his airways.

Chris and I weren't sleeping–only catching half-nights of rest. One of us would wake the other to take the next shift, holding our baby boy upright so he could breath and hopefully get some rest so his little body could recover. The medications altered his personality, and I watched in heartbreak as his eyes became glossy and the loving baby we once knew became distant.

I pleaded with his pediatrician for a glimmer of hope, to which she replied, "Stay the course. Hopefully he outgrows this respiratory response by age five." By *AGE FIVE?!!* The poison we were giving him daily would likely leave him so debilitated that we would have many other major health concerns on the table. It was the first time I ever cried out to God *in anger*, "Why aren't You answering my prayers?! Don't You hear me? Don't you care? Do whatever You want to me, but heal my baby boy!"

My unbelief deep down surfaced again through my current suffering. I brought to Jesus all I had: anger, pain, frustration, and fear. And guess what? He not only could bear it, He used it as a backdrop to prove His goodness and love toward me and my family.

Paul Tripp says, "Suffering exposes you. It exposes what you think about life and God. You bring a whole package to the way that you suffer. God knew we needed help with suffering. The Bible pictures a world of suffering. It gives us a different way to think about why we suffer, who God is in suffering, and what He offers us through it. It demonstrates that suffering is not in the way of God's plan–it's part of God's plan.[1]

Just a couple of weeks after my prayer of desperation, a sweet friend humbly asked if we'd ever considered testing our son for allergies at a more natural practice. We didn't have the money to go off the beaten path of Western medicine, which was all our insurance covered. In seemingly one fell swoop, we joined a Christian medical-sharing group, had our son tested, and he was diagnosed with over 25 allergies, both environmental and food-related. He began sublingual immunotherapy, and we did our best to control his exposure to allergens.

With this combined treatment, he never had another airway inflammation attack. Within four months he was off all medications and back to his fun-loving self. By that time, our baby girl had joined the family, and our new Christian medical-sharing group covered everything over the initial $300 of both his treatment AND her birth. We not only felt seen by God, but we also felt surrounded by His goodness and favor.

When I invited Him into our suffering, He showed up in a way that made it undeniable–He was indeed *for* us. We learned that He would fight for us in the midst of our fears and remain present with us in our suffering.

This wasn't the end of our boy's health journey. His bones were brittle from the overuse of steroids, and he broke his leg twice in one summer from simple movements. He spent over a month relearning to walk at age five. For the next couple of years, his ability to focus on his schoolwork was nearly impossible. Just months later, he developed bizarre symptoms. My mom and sister, thankfully, had read about these symptoms and urged us to have him checked out.

After consulting with a dear friend and medical professional, we took him first thing in the morning to test his blood sugar.

"Type 1 Diabetes", the doctor said after a quick finger poke. I could tell by the doctor's fallen countenance and the deep compassion in his voice that it was serious. "What is it?" I asked, voice quivering while I held my frail boy in my lap.

"It's an autoimmune disease. He needs immediate medical attention. He will not live without it. I'll call the hospital and tell them you're on your way. I'm so sorry."

Our world turned upside down–again. The grief that comes from your child's safety being threatened is undeniably the hardest grief to bear, second only to the death of a child. Our boy was not dead, but according to the medical staff, he would have been in a matter of days had we not brought him in. We grieved that reality. *How could we not see that he was dying??* We were afraid, but this time, nothing in us questioned God's goodness. We just knew He would show up. How? We had no clue. But when we had no way to make things better, He became our everything. Our every hope was secured in Him alone.

Looking back, we can see it. Pictures of him standing by our kiddie pool in his swim trunks reveal each of his ribs exposed. His cheeks were sunken in. He was constantly starving and thirsty, eating and drinking himself sick. He began bedwetting and felt nauseated off and on for months. We know now that infection in his cells, combined with the toll of illness and harsh medications earlier in his life, threw him into autoimmunity.

I could write another book about our health journeys and all we've learned, but I'll wrap it up with this: God proved His *goodness* amidst our previous struggle. Now, He was proving *His nearness in this one*.

Every time suffering has come into our lives, God uses it to secure our faith in supernatural ways that withstand future trials. He uses suffering to shape an unwavering faith that couldn't be constructed apart from it.

Our son has a couple of expensive "robot parts" that keep him healthy and alive, monitoring his blood sugar levels and injecting life-saving insulin around the clock. But he is alive. And because of medical advancements over the last 100 years, he can live a life full of as much adventure as he can dream up. *Thank You, Jesus*.

Do we still have to keep surrendering his health and future wellbeing with this autoimmune response? We for sure do. It's not easy. But Psalm 37 reminds us to not give way to fear. *Biblical faith will never ask us to deny reality*. But we look at reality through the lens of the power and presence of God. Delight in the Lord, and He will act. Verse 18 says He is near to the brokenhearted and saves the crushed in spirit. We feel this every time things get tough, and we are reminded to surrender. Because as human beings, fallen to sin, it's very hard for us to imagine someone who is perfectly loving and always does the right thing no matter the situation or temptation. *Yet this is who Jesus is*.

Most people in the midst of suffering don't want an academic answer–they want Jesus. They want someone to be like Jesus to them. They want a Father who loves them in the midst of their trials. The fact is, God didn't create evil and suffering. Love requires a choice: to love or not to love. He gave us free will, and we chose not to love. We chose to walk away from God. We brought evil and suffering into the world. But He didn't leave us without hope. He offers eternity with Him, absent of suffering. And while we're still here on earth, He sent Jesus Christ to redeem mankind. He will use the difficulties of our life to draw out good, to bring people into His Kingdom, sharpen our character, and cultivate perseverance.[2]

If you've ever doubted the goodness of God, as I have, in a moment when you were experiencing something that didn't seem right, I pray this chapter feels like a healing balm on your soul. Evil and suffering are not contrary to the story of the Bible.

"Christianity makes sense of, gives meaning to, and offers a solution for the evil and suffering we experience."

–Craig Groeschel

Craig Groeschel points out that the Bible doesn't avoid pain, evil, and suffering. Jeremiah, known as the weeping prophet–cries out to God in pain because God's people would not turn to Him. David, "a man after God's own heart," asks, "Are you even listening, God? Do You even care?" John the Baptist, whose sole purpose was to prepare for the coming of the Messiah, is wrongly arrested and beheaded. Jesus could have come and saved him, but He didn't. John likely sat in that prison cell and wondered where God was.

Groeschel states that "if love is a choice, suffering is a possibility. The only way that love is possible is if we have the choice to choose it. Free will is the ability to choose. If you have the ability to choose love, you also have the ability to choose hate. Similarly, if you have the ability to choose good, you have the ability to choose evil. God gave us free will because He didn't want robots–He wanted us to be able to choose to love Him. For God to remove pain and suffering, He would either have to remove love or remove us. If there were no God, who would there be to say what is right or wrong? The fact that we believe in evil and suffering is evidence that we believe God exists." [3]

To live a life in awe of and reverence to what our God can do is the fear of the Lord. He is indeed a good God, and He is for us. When we reverently fear the Lord, we fear nothing else.

"The fear of the Lord is a fountain of life, that one may turn away from the snares of death."
—Proverbs 14:27

The morning after I was raped in a hotel room, I returned to the safety of my childhood home, doing my best to act normal and maintain the lie that I had been at an NJROTC lock-in all night. My Mom expected me to be tired, so it didn't raise any alarms when I wanted to go straight to my room to rest. Closing my bedroom door, I was safe to let my guard down. But all I wanted to do was disappear. My purpose for existence was completely shaken. *Who was I now? How long can I maintain the appearance that I have it all together? What does that even mean... "having it all together?" I'm an imposter. I don't belong anywhere. No one will accept me. God doesn't accept me.*

I was 40 years old before I could make any sense of what actually happened to me at age 14. One night, after my husband and three young children had gone to bed, I was reading through testimonies of sex trafficking survivors. It was 2021, and an explosion of stories and ministries to help these victims had come into public view via social media platforms.

Each one was like a horrible wreck I couldn't bring myself to look away from. I felt awful for these women and couldn't imagine what it would be like to live through such trauma.

Although I had been reading stories off and on for a couple of months, this night was different. As I read one woman's story, the details resonated with me… deeply. I couldn't even tell you now what the details were, but I remember goosebumps from head to toe and a sinking feeling in my stomach. Immediately, I prayed aloud, *"God, please don't tell me sex trafficking is part of my story! That's too much!"*

His response was immediate and gentle, reminding me that I didn't need faith for the whole journey in that moment–just enough for the next step of obedience. Remember, God wants our whole hearts, and His timing in bringing the truth to the surface is perfect. Never before would I have had the relational space or time to face the reality of the trauma I had lived through. But after physically moving away from everything our family of five knew, I held absolutely everything with open hands and was very protective of what my family chose to lean into.

As a homeschool mom, I have a lot of influence over the bulk of home life. We weren't going to fill our days with mere busyness–only pursuits and relationships that served God's purposes for us would be allowed to take our energy. Of course, I haven't always known what this looks like, but He has faithfully shown up and led us every day.

Healing from past hurt was at the top of the priority list when we moved in August 2019. Because of necessity, we immediately jumped into renovating our fixer-upper home in the St. Louis area while trying to acclimate to our new church family during a time when the world seemed flipped upside down and community was very difficult to come by. Jesus kept our circle small, while space to heal and hear His voice was plentiful. Little did I know just how comprehensive He would prove in my healing journey.

That night on the couch, I sat in silence, wrestling with the possibility that I had been groomed by a trafficking ring. I asked Jesus what He wanted me to do. His response was simple: before going to bed, I was to send an email to the ministry that had posted the girl's testimony and request to speak with someone.

One week later, I was on the phone with a young lady from the ministry who was herself a survivor of sex trafficking. Miraculously, she now walks alongside others, offering clarity, hope, and resources to women with similar trauma. "Was this even happening in the late 1990s?" I asked her. "Absolutely," she responded. "This has been going on for decades but it used to be viewed as prostitution–as a crime women willingly participated in. Only in the last few years has there been tremendous work in exposing it for what it really is: modern-day slavery."

I shared my story with her, but not in the way I had been telling it for nearly a decade. This time, I shared with her the details that didn't make sense to me, as the Holy Spirit led me to do so. He tenderly gave me the ability to recall details and bravely invite this sister in Christ into things I had never before said out loud The fact that different guys would come and pick me up in the middle of the night while I was still in a relationship with my "boyfriend." The disorientation of always being brought to a different location, which left me feeling uneasy. The constant pressure to perform and initiate sex. The utterly demoralizing nature of being raped with others in the room–no one coming to my rescue–as if it were normal to everyone except me. These were the details that came to mind as I shared without even trying hard to remember them. It was as if they were just waiting to be brought into the light.

The young woman, barely in her twenties, responded with grace and clarity well beyond her years. "Although each story is different, there are tell-tale signs of trafficking, and your story has them. In the grooming phase of trafficking, the victim is introduced to several men. Each of these men would have likely raped you in the next phases of being inducted into the trafficking ring. The reason you were brought to different locations was to make disorientation your new norm. I think Uncle Mikey was the pimp. And after hearing your story, I believe the fact that you came from a loving home, along with your faith in God, were what made you a *difficult target*."

Her words pierced through the confusion, plainly revealing God's protection of me in the most vulnerable, despairing time of my life.

She went on to explain how trafficking rings want to remain in the darkness. They operate in the middle of a city without drawing attention to themselves. She was right–my family would've come looking for me had I never returned home. They loved me. And the Holy Spirit in me caused me to ask *real* questions… to notice the shell of a woman in the corner of the room and not look away, to not just stay silent while a man old enough to be my father forced himself on me. The light in my heart and life threatened to expose this darkness. And all glory to goes Jesus because it was Him who shone His light in me. He said, "I began a work in you, Crystal, and I am going to complete it, even in the face of opposition."

Parents, we make our children difficult targets by cultivating a relationship with them that's counter-cultural. Don't settle for letting everyone else raise your child–whether in person or through a screen. We've been given the privilege of discipling them and leading them through these most tender years of development. If you work outside the home and send your kids to school, you will have less time to do this, but it *is* possible. Be intentional about the time you do have with them.

Though the responsibility to steward these years is ours alone, God didn't create us to go it alone. Finding a healthy church family to come alongside you as you raise your children is life-giving and necessary. We all benefit greatly from the support and care the body of Christ offers. Make space for it. Don't have a healthy church community? Cultivate one. Chris and I have found Jesus to be enough in both the plenty and in the lacking when it comes to healthy community. In times when it has been scarce, He has invited us to simply live it out as we lean on Him for all we need, invite others to join us. We all want people with whom we can be real–no one wants another circle to perform for. The reality is, we're all broken and in need of a Savior. All day every day. How hard is it to invite someone into *that*? No fronts, no filters. It takes so much less energy and effort to just be real.

Our children look to us to help them discover who they were created to be. They need help and encouragement to embrace their purpose. If we're honest, we as parents struggle to keep our own purpose in view when making decisions. A community that loves Jesus and loves our family is an integral part of helping us see the blind spots that would lead us down a dangerous path of isolation and self-preservation.

As our kids grow, they will thrive under the protection of a home that is living in reckless abandon to what the world deems "normal." This doesn't ensure they won't struggle or experience pain and heartache, but it does set our family up to be held by His loving arms when we don't have the strength to stand. It helps us navigate everything–from sleepless nights with a newborn, to trying times with teens, to life as empty nesters.

Children who know their worth–because it's communicated to them through everyday interactions–will not need to look elsewhere in search for it. *The very best way we can protect our kids is from the inside out.* Teach them who they are and Whose they are. And if you don't know it for yourself, it's time to lean in and let it completely change you as you heal from past hurt and pain. *Jesus knows the way.*

CHAPTER 12

WHO IS HE IN MY SUFFERING

I made a commitment to Jesus that I would no longer hide away the hard stuff. I haven't been aimless in sharing, though. I recognized, soon after He specifically called me to surrender my entire story for His purposes, that fear would creep in. Constantly. The thing is, it was such a familiar companion to me that I didn't even know it was there. It was causing unnecessary suffering. As we've already discussed, fear isn't a bad thing when we allow it to move us toward Jesus. With a new understanding of the role fear ought to play in my life, I used it as a catalyst to pray that God would bring me the person with whom He wanted me to share my story. The crazy thing is–He did.

Every single time I've felt that all-too-familiar fear creeping in, causing my mind and body to immediately feel threatened, followed by the overpowering urge to push away and shut down, I pray. With the frailest amount of expectation, I look to Jesus with a faith that's desperate to grow beyond the constraints of the mere details that make up my story. With each prayer, Jesus has provided. I soon realized that as I bring my fear to Him, *He turns it into an opportunity* for healing.

The beautiful thing about Jesus is when we leave things up to Him, His creations are far better than anything we could hope or imagine. This is what I want for you and for any woman He puts in my circle. I simply learned to obediently call upon Him for my own healing. He's blessed that beyond belief with an opportunity for me to walk other women to do the same, in my Healing D.E.E.P.E.R. online community. For more on my Healing D.E.E.P.E.R. community crystalpersons.com/healing-deeper.com.

The women He has brought to me have been searching too–also in need of a safe space, a listening ear, and a hope they could rest in as they learn to journey forward from past trauma. But the primary focus of sharing my story has been *my own healing*. Jesus draws near. I surrender. He calls. I obey. He guides and equips. I heal and am made strong through my weakness. Sweet, glorious redemption of all I once counted lost.

There have also been many times I've shared my story in the context of small groups with my brothers and sisters in Christ. I remember the first time I shared with men present–it terrified me. I had no clue how they would respond, but subconsciously, I *needed* them to speak into my trauma. When they, together with the women in the room, met me with so much grace and even protectiveness, it began healing a place deep inside me that still believed I would be entirely rejected if anyone really knew about my past. When my brothers and sisters together spoke into my story, the enemy was silenced. I could tell, all at once, the lies that were his, apart from the truth of who Jesus was calling me to be.

Jesus' calling is holistic. He wants all of me. And He wants every bit of you too. What He would do with our surrender–of all we know and all we are–radically blows the cover off the tactics the enemy uses to keep us from walking in true freedom.

Although suffering is part of living in a broken world, there is a way in which we suffer that leads to life and freedom, no matter the circumstances. Sometimes we have the ability to influence our suffering, and sometimes we must endure it. Understanding the reasons why we suffer gives us clarity on how we approach the throne of grace and move forward.

Suffering that you can influence happens when you're living in perpetual, unconfessed sin, which only brings destruction upon yourself and those who love you. Your relationships will undoubtedly be marked with pain and strife. Unfortunately, your pride can keep you trapped, always believing the lie that it's everyone else who is to blame for the dysfunction in your life. But when the common denominator in all your broken relationships is you, pausing to pray for your eyes to be opened to your self-destructive ways is a necessary first step.

The amazing, grace-filled news is that for those who are born again, Jesus's posture toward you is one of pursuit and grace. He literally leaves the ninety-nine and chases after the one who is lost. He will bring correction and discipline into your life over and over again to draw you back to His heart. *He desires intimate community with you.* You may have chosen to leave Him, but He has not left you. He is ready to forgive you and welcome you back to His side. And He will use His body to facilitate reconciliation and redemption of all things broken and lost.

Suffering you don't have much influence over and must endure occurs when someone sins against us personally. This doesn't mean that you are a doormat to their sin and abuse, but you don't hold the power to change others. Depending on the nature of the relationship, the season of enduring may be short or much longer than you feel you can possibly bear on your own. If the one who has sinned against you is quick to ask forgiveness and also right the wrongs they incurred when they sinned against you, restoration of the relationship can begin and trust can start to be rebuilt. Keep in mind, if the sin against you is especially deep and dark, reconciliation will not happen overnight. Often, counseling, accountability measures (ideally from a trusted loved one other than the one who was wronged), and clear boundaries are necessary throughout the reconciliation process. As uncomfortable as it is, genuine restoration of relationships that have undergone hurt takes time.

What about when the one who sinned against you is stuck in their sin and pride? Here is a life-giving nugget of truth I wish I had grasped years ago: when the individual who sinned against you refuses to take ownership of their sin, you are under *no biblical responsibility* to forgive them. Sound radical? Unbiblical, even?? It did to me too.

Having grown up in the church, I've heard time and time again that we *must* forgive, no matter what, even if the individual never asks for our forgiveness. Dr. Gary Chapman, author of *The 5 Languages of Apology*, challenged this thinking at a recent conference at our church by stating that the Bible never tells us to forgive someone who isn't asking for our forgiveness. In fact, Dr. Chapman rightly points out that not even God forgives us without us asking for His forgiveness. Romans 5:8 says that while we were still sinners, Christ died for us, but it doesn't say He forgave sinners.

Does this entire concept feel utterly wrong? What if it merely goes against what you (and I) have learned? As always, let's test it with Scripture.

"If we confess our sins, He is faithful and just to forgive us our sins and to cleanse us from all unrighteousness." –1 John 1:9

"If your brother sins, rebuke him, and if he repents, forgive him, and if he sins against you seven times in the day, and turns to you seven times, saying, 'I repent,' you must forgive him." –Luke 17:3-4

"For you, O Lord, are good and forgiving, abounding in steadfast love to all who call upon you." –Psalm 86:5

There are many other passages on forgiveness in the Bible, but none indicate that forgiveness hasn't already been asked by the one who sinned…

"He has delivered us from the domain of darkness and transferred us to the Kingdom of His beloved Son, in whom we have redemption, the forgiveness of sins." –Colossians 1:13-14

"Whoever covers an offense seeks love, but he who repeats a matter separates close friends." –Proverbs 17:9

"For if you forgive others their trespasses, your heavenly Father will also forgive you, but if you do not forgive others their trespasses, neither will your Father forgive your trespasses." –Matthew 6:14-15

So then, what are you to do when someone sins against you and does not ask for your forgiveness? *You release them to God.* This is paramount in our personal healing. We cannot allow the sin of another to hold us captive. When we release them to God, we are laying their offenses at His feet and trusting Jesus to bring that person to repentance. We wait for Him to bring justice for the harm done against us. This doesn't excuse their sin, but it removes our need to wait for their apology before we can begin healing. This is how we walk in freedom amidst wickedness.

An important note is that whether or not the person asks your forgiveness, trust is only restored as the individual who sinned works to rebuild it. We are not commanded to trust others in the Bible, as I have mentioned in a recent chapter. God alone is ever worthy of our trust. He would never ask you to trust someone who has hurt you and broken your trust. Biblically, trusting someone who has proven untrustworthy is unwise and not how you walk together with God in truth.

Although they may manipulatively tell you otherwise, rebuilding trust is a key element to the restoration of a broken relationship, and the burden of this work falls squarely on the one who has sinned. You may need to ask Jesus for help in receiving their efforts to rebuild your trust, but don't allow unnecessary suffering by shouldering more than what Jesus is calling you to bear in a strained relationship.

Yet another way we suffer is because of the general effects of sin in a fallen world. Illness, natural disasters, corrupt governments and leaders, disease, and death are all a part of life because sin is present in the world. It's devastating. There's no one to point the finger at (you know you would have messed up had you been in Adam and Eve's spot, and I would have too), and it's impossible to make sense of it. Collectively, even nature itself groans for Jesus' return: *"For we know that the whole creation has been groaning together in the pains of childbirth until now."* (Romans 8:22)

The apostle Paul also wrote that *"the sufferings of this present time are not worth comparing with the glory that is to be revealed to us."* (Romans 8:18) A tension exists between present sufferings and future glory. We do not yet see this glory, for it must be revealed at the appointed time.

With all the reasons for suffering other than personal sin (because the ball is in our own court with that one), how should we respond as God's people? Well, we have a *personal relationship* with the one and only Healer, Comforter, and Redeemer Himself. This means we can not only navigate personal hurt, but we can also lead our culture in a healthy response to suffering.

Imagine how different our nation would look if we shined His glorious light into the darkness as opposed to allowing the darkness to lead the conversation, influence the hashtags, and embody a cultural response to suffering. Darkness has been masquerading as light since the beginning of history, and our culture embraces it without pause for the havoc and sheer destruction left in its wake. This is why we are in the mess we are in as a nation. We have looked to a lost world in the midst of confusing times, and the enemy gladly took the lead, brazenly outlining how we should walk and talk. The result has been more isolation, fear, and confusion than before.

It is imperative that we lean into community that submits to the perfect authority of Jesus Christ. In the midst of suffering, He leads with clarity, freedom, and peace, restoring what's broken and redeeming what's lost. He is the very Author of healing and truth. He shows us through suffering how to take our broken selves and make an eternal difference in the world around us.

You might say in response to all this, *"But I've been hurt by so-called Christians. I simply cannot invite them or anyone else into my suffering and pain."*

Unfortunately, the church can be a place that brings further suffering to individuals. Paul David Tripp says, "It's very easy to throw spiritual platitudes at [those who are suffering]. That's different than incarnating those truths in the way that you respond to the person. Ask yourself, 'How do I make the truth of God's nearness become real in being near to people?' Don't give a drive by 'God's near.' *Be the theology* that you are preaching to people. Don't just preach it from a distance."

Chris and I have been in ministry for twenty years and have been humans for well over forty. We both grew up in the church and have experienced personal suffering on a multitude of levels. One thing that always makes the pain of suffering nearly unbearable is when well-meaning but misunderstanding fellow believers say, *"Maybe you're struggling so much because you're harboring unforgiveness."*

If you find yourself suffering as the result of another's sin, know that this response doesn't communicate the heart of God toward you in your suffering. Remember, the burden of taking ownership of sin and rebuilding trust belongs solely to the one who has sinned against you. Until this process of Biblical reconciliation begins, you will feel pain and might even struggle to gain your footing as you wait on God to do what only He can do. You will need your brothers and sisters to bear up under this burden with you for a season.

Do you need to stay vigilant so that a hard heart doesn't develop toward the one who wronged you? Of course. But is the *only* possible reason you're struggling because you have a hard, sinful heart toward them? Absolutely not. This is simply an unseasoned view by those who have not yet suffered for long periods of time at the hand of another. I can say this so bluntly because it used to be me.

Early on in ministry, I didn't know how to face my sorrow and grief. I gave people a very short time to "suffer" before offering my unsolicited counsel and judgment: "Maybe you are suffering because of, well…*you*." My heart sinks even as I type this.

If you are reading this as someone hurt by my immature and prideful response during personal suffering, I am deeply sorry. Please forgive me. I was wrong. My head knowledge had not made its way down into the depths of my heart. I was too busy guarding my own heart from being exposed and hurt again to see what you truly needed most…someone to embody Christ by walking compassionately with you through painful and disorienting territory.

We as the church are too quick to rush past people's hurt because it's just plain uncomfortable for us to sit in their mourning booth with them. We don't have the words. We don't understand. We tire quickly of the weightiness and pain. The constant longing for reconciliation, meaning, justice, or healing doesn't make for light-hearted coffee conversation.

What's wrong with them? Why can't they just move on? Surely their prolonged suffering is sinful.

There are many reasons why someone would suffer for an extended period of time. Health concerns for oneself or a loved one can feel like a moment-by-moment faith walk. Some health threats are visible and obvious, while others are only seen by those very close to the individual. Many will never be physically healed this side of heaven. That's a tremendously heavy burden to carry.

Loss of a loved one ushers in unimaginable grief that becomes a constant companion. Keeping their memory alive becomes a necessary tool in survival, and the deep longing for meaning seems insatiable. Learning to enjoy life in a way that honors the life lost weighs heavy as each new day comes. Mere pity doesn't ease the pain, but a listening ear and a warm hug can embody Jesus' nearness in their grief and loss.

Another reason for prolonged suffering is abuse. Sometimes it's visible to others; other times, it's concealed in utter darkness. Abuse takes many forms–physical, domestic, sexual, psychological or emotional, financial or material, organizational or institutional, and even spiritual. If a person is actively in an abusive relationship or situation, they are taking a tremendous personal risk to invite you in. The path out of the situation may not be clear to them. They need help. *They need a safe space.*

PTSD also causes extended suffering, and is not at all linear. As discussed in the first chapter, actual alterations of the brain occur during trauma to protect itself. Parts of the brain shut down and shrink over time, while other parts became overactive and incredibly sensitive to anything that would trigger a similar feeling or experience of the trauma.

With all this suffering within and around us, those who have endured suffering because of things outside of their control are a much-needed salve within the church body. These people know how necessary just being present with the sufferer demonstrates that God is there in the midst of their suffering. They remind the sufferer that He is tender and will not forsake them in their time of need. They listen to understand the deep churnings of the soul, making space for Jesus to begin the long process of healing. And if reconciliation never comes, those who have suffered at the feet of Jesus know how to offer tangible hope to others who are suffering.

Have you been through some things? Have you seen God prove worthy of your trust during a time when you were wrongly accused? Have you known Him deeply as a perfect portion in all things? If the answer to these questions is "yes", the body of Christ needs you.

"God makes His invisible grace visible by sending people of grace to give grace to people who need grace. Be one of those people."

–Paul David Tripp[1]

We cannot escape it. Suffering is a part of life and will affect us. *Suffering reveals what we have our hope in*. When we suffer as a result of another's sin against us, or because of the effects of sin in the world, Jesus positions Himself right next to us:. *"The Lord is near to the brokenhearted and saves the crushed in spirit."* (Psalm 34:18)

Understanding God's posture towards the sufferer is everything. He is not judging. He is not dismissive.

He is not condemning. He is not angry. He is not turning His back. *He is near.*

Take a moment to let that sink in–*in our brokenness, Jesus is near.* It is not a sin to be broken. Sin creates a barrier. Sin separates. Sin does not bring closeness but causes distance in relationships. If Jesus is drawing near to the brokenhearted, it means that the one who is broken is not living in unconfessed sin.

Jesus drawing near also means that He is offering protection. It means He is *for* the brokenhearted. It means that the things that are breaking the heart of the sufferer are breaking Jesus' heart too.

His close proximity means He knows you're going to need Him every single moment. He's within reach, and He has a purpose for your brokenness. He wants to redeem every single thing that comes against you. He is fighting on your behalf so that it is *His truth* that reigns in the midst of the struggle, and the enemy is silenced. When our hearts are broken for the things that break His heart, we are mobilized in battle alongside Him, fighting against the darkness. We cannot sit still, nor can we be silent. We've seen too much. We've felt the devastation first hand. There is no going back to how things were before. Freedom, hope, and *life* are at stake. And because our hearts have been broken by the effects of sin, we fight. *We fight* for ourselves, and, moved with holy compassion, we fight for others.

Dr. Paul Tripp teaches that "lament has its purpose in suffering as well. It reminds me that He would never leave me in a broken world by myself. Brokenness is going to enter our door. The Bible never asks you to deny your emotions. Biblical faith never asks you to deny reality. Isn't that encouraging? We crave to know if anyone cares, if anyone understands. Jesus says, *"Cast your cares on Me because I care for you."* Hebrews tells us we have a sympathetic and understanding High Priest. God understands our humanity. The deepest moment of Jesus' pain on the cross wasn't physical–it was emotional. He has a full, experiential understanding of what we're going through. The move of God's grace isn't from dependence to independence, but from independence to dependence. And that's where we find hope. *Hopelessness is the failure of what I put my hope in. Jesus cannot fail.*"[2]

So, what are we supposed to do with our suffering, with our sorrow and grief? Denial of our reality and numbness to it are the ethos of our culture. We don't even question if that's how we're supposed to live our lives. But the cost is isolation.

Connection happens when we are vulnerable and let people into the areas of our life that aren't shiny evidences of our successes and growth. We must risk sharing our heartache if we are going to have genuine community, which is necessary for our health and healing from past hurts. When we hide our sorrow and grief from others, and from ourselves, there is no place for it to go. When they cannot be brought out into the light, very bad things happen to the human heart and body.

What conditions are needed to allow our sorrow and grief to heal? First, we need to own that our sorrows and griefs matter and that they should be taken seriously. We need to gradually move from a posture of contempt toward our sorrow and grief to a posture of compassion. We need to find a few people who can be our village, allowing us to risk sharing vulnerably with others.

I submit to you that Jesus is the Author of our healing. He knows how to bring each and every detail into place so we can begin healing, and He can functionally redeem our hurt for His eter*nal purposes. Dr. Adam Young* paraphrases it well: we need to metabolize our hurt. Jeremiah 6:14 & 8:11 (NIV) says, *"you dress the wounds of My people as if they are not serious, you say 'peace, peace' but there is no peace."* We often forego addressing the hard things within us because we are afraid of the depth of our sorrow. We tell ourselves we're okay and that we don't need to heal. Isaiah 63:8-10 says that in all Israel's distress, God, too, was distressed, yet they rebelled and grieved His Spirit. God feels grief and sorrow, and He is holy. So, we know that it is actually holy to grieve.

Let us then, as God's people, be set apart from cultural norms and make space to heal in such a way that cultivates freedom from oppression. (If you're looking for a safe space to heal, head to crystalpersons.com/free-resources where I provide many free ways to process, be supported, and to step into your healing journey.)

"For freedom Christ has set us free; stand firm therefore, and do not submit again to a yoke of slavery...for through the Spirit, by faith, we ourselves eagerly wait for the hope of righteousness. For in Christ neither circumcision nor uncircumcision counts for anything, but only faith working through love...you were called to freedom, brothers. Only do not use your freedom as an opportunity for the flesh, but through love serve one another. If we live by the Spirit, let us also keep in step with the Spirit." (excerpts from Galatians 5)

PART 5

EMBRACE NEW DEPTHS

CHAPTER 13

TIME WITH HIM

Do you come into His presence seeking?

As I open God's Word, I simply pray and ask Him to lead me through it. It's literally what He does–He leads us in spirit and in truth. One of the works of the Holy Spirit is to illuminate our minds to understand the depths of God's character and heart as it pertains to what we are walking through moment by moment.

The Bible is not an ancient, irrelevant manuscript that belongs on a shelf, nightstand, or coffee table, only to be referenced when we feel like accumulating more head knowledge. His Word is *living* and *breathing*, actively and rightly dividing the very truth that sets us free from the lies that deceive and ensnare us. And because the Holy Spirit resides in those who call Jesus their Savior and Lord, He guides us through God's written Word. We don't need a seminary degree to understand the depths of His love for us, nor do we need the title of pastor or teacher to grasp His pursuit of us in the day-to-day.

He will use Genesis through Revelation to endear our hearts anew to His work in our midst–*if indeed we are seeking Him*. The question is, do you come into His presence *seeking*? What is your heart posture when you open His Word and talk with Him throughout the day? Is it one of surrender and expectation? Or are you hurried, simply checking the box, hoping the mere ritual of daily reading His Word somehow makes a difference?

Maybe you aren't even cracking open the Word of truth on a regular basis. Perhaps you feel hopeless or fairly certain that spending time with God isn't going to change a thing. You believe *you* have to make things happen. *You* must maintain control.

I have fallen into each of these categories throughout my life. I can tell you with all certainty that only one heart posture cultivates freedom: *surrender*. Allowing my current reality to give way to the truth of who He is, and who He says I am, over and over and over again. His work is always a new work, and so we must not let our current understanding put limitations on Him. Instead, we must lean in to know His heart anew, to see how our current reality weaves together with His plan.

Healing from brokenness and past trauma frees us up. And with this new capacity to dream, hope, and plan for the future, we must remain plugged into the true power source–God. With thousands of years to study mankind, the enemy knows that if simply bringing something "good" to occupy our time will distract us from walking in dependence on the One who sets us free, then he'll do just that. The attack is often subtle, and before we know it, we are bound up and enslaved once again.

Experiencing God first hand is the only way to ensure freedom moving forward. Knowing His heart isn't confusing if we're in His Word. A simple practice I've adopted over the years is to read a chapter or a section of Scripture and pray that the Holy Spirit would open my eyes to what He has for me to know and do based on what I just read. When a passage sticks out to me, I pause and ask Jesus *why* it caught my attention. I reread the verses that caught my attention, asking Him what He wants me to understand. Then I personalize the verse through prayer.

I have an example of this process at the end of the chapter. It's how my brain works, so it's how He meets with *me*. Use this model if it helps you experience Him more deeply, or use another method like a reading plan and devotional combo, such as *The Bible Recap*. But whatever you do, don't fall into the trap of needing certain things in place in order to experience the reality of His presence in your life. Don't try to contain the God of the universe within the limits of your human understanding.

Throughout college, I relied on devotionals that led me through specific passages of Scripture, then provided questions to help me apply the truths I'd just read. It softened my heart and renewed my mind. When I lived a year in Peru, I read the Word and journaled my prayers daily. I also used sweet little notecards Chris made up to help me stay connected to Jesus while I was away. Each little card had a spot to record something from the passage of Scripture I read and followed the A.C.T.S. acronym: *Adoration* of a character trait of God's that was meaningful to me that day, *Confession* of sins, *Thanksgiving* for evidence of His work, and *Supplication*–laying my requests at His feet for myself and others.

In the years since–through marriage, ministry, kids, homeschooling, moving, T1D and PANDAS diagnoses, renovating our home, loss of loved ones, illnesses, becoming Airbnb hosts, maintaining social media accounts, and now writing a book–my methods of connecting with God have changed. A lot.

I spent years thinking that I wasn't *really* meeting with Him if I didn't have a pen and journal in hand. I carried so much guilt because of that belief. But the fact is, Jesus doesn't need us to come with loads of time and scholar-level mental capacity. He simply tells us to *come*, and He will give us rest.

Come burdened.
Come happy.
Come angry.
Come sleepy.
Come with a full heart.
Come depleted.
Come frustrated.
Come thankful.

Come grieving.
Come searching.

Just come to Him wherever you are. Come seeking, and you will find Him.

My posture in coming to Him is what sets the tone for the encounter. Because I grew up knowing I needed to read the Bible and pray–because it's what good Christians do–I constantly have to challenge my default setting. Maybe I struggle with this because I find comfort in guidelines: *tell me what to do so I know I'm on the right track and within the confines of approval.* (People-pleaser, anyone?)

I have to actively and ruthlessly deprogram the "check-the-box, look-the-part" Christianity because it's man-made slavery, serving a mere idol of Christ-followers who appear to have their stuff together. I want a radical, even-if-I-just-have-time- to-touch-the-hem-of-His-garment kind of faith that is desperate for Him. Come as I am–*expectant* to experience Him in a way that changes my everything.

It's not about what I bring to Him. He doesn't need my pen or my highlighters or my journal. Are they helpful tools to keep me focused as I dive in to study and understand what I'm reading? Sure, they are. But are they a necessary part of me abiding in His grace and walking in His power for the day? Absolutely not. *Just come.*

I believe *comfort* is the biggest attack on us North Americans experiencing Jesus authentically. We are inundated by superficial means to cope with the pain and emptiness we feel on any given day. We are easily pacified by food, entertainment, and selfish pleasures, while being numbed by copious amounts of empty input from our phones, social media, and streaming services. Why would we choose to live in the reality of our desperation and neediness when we don't have to? Escapism is robbing us blind.

This summer alone has brought more heartache and struggles than my family of five could possibly bear on our own. My sister passed away unexpectedly at the beginning of July. She was only 48 years old. We are still awaiting the autopsy report, but the leading cause was heart failure. Her death sent my family into a spiral of emotions as we tried to hold one another from hours apart until we could physically be together for the funeral. Chris, with his shepherd's heart, graciously officiated an intimate ceremony. It was a beautiful gift for us to have that closure together.

Just 3 days after news of my sister's passing, our youngest was diagnosed with PANDAS–a strep infection in her brain that has been wreaking havoc on her neurological system since she was a newborn. I also lost one of my two beehives to maggots, even though I had worked hard, this being my first year as a beekeeper, to multiply them and produce a honey harvest. *Maggots y'all. Gross!*

A week after returning home, we faced an abrupt and odd attack on our family that was highly disorienting, especially as our minds were still very much struggling to get back to "normal" life after the funeral. It was an isolated situation, and we thankfully had the support we needed to get through it. Even still, we grieve the loss of friendship and are frustrated by what was clearly the enemy causing such unnecessary hardship.

Then, severe pneumonia hit our home. Although it was nearly a month ago, we are still working to get two of our kids up and healthy again. All of this has left us…desperate. Frazzled. Uncertain. Needy.

Enter Jesus–the only One who can truly satisfy–while we face off with more than we could ever muscle through, even on a good day. When we simply come to Him with heavy hearts and more burdens than we could possibly bear, He shows up and proves He is every bit of who He says He is in the pages of His Word.

He has begun redeeming my family of origin, bringing unity through a love that put everything else aside as we showed up for one another. With the brevity of life staring us in the face, we now find time to be present in one another's lives and work through things we've shelved for far too long. Our church family and friends brought us meals, cried with us, prayed over us, checked in, and showed up. They folded laundry, tidied up, spent time with the kids so they could just be kids in the midst of heaviness, helped with the huge task of hair days, and loved us fiercely.

Our sweet neighbors brought us Indian tea countless times. Another let us swim in their pool in between all the crazy. And another got the most darling little puppy, and, together with their sweet kids, have brought so much happiness to our girls. *God moved people* to remind us, both in our waking and sleeping, that He is ever so near.

This reality stands true: we experience the abundance of His provision, love, and grace when we are depleted of our own means to change our circumstances. When we must face the hardest things, we cry out, and He proves worthy. So, we are convinced that circumstantial comfort directly opposes the intimate experience of the God of comfort.

When was the last time you were forced to come face-to-face with the reality of your desperate need for Jesus to show up? How did it grow your faith? What is superficially pacifying you or even numbing you from the reality He's calling you to walk in with Him?

The thing is, when we authentically experience God, we heal. And when we begin healing, Jesus grows our capacity. What should we do with this new freedom and capacity? We must steward it, allowing Jesus to multiply the work He's doing within us so others may also be set free–so they can be set free *through our testimony.*

The key to more is stewarding what we already have well. I used to think I could handle more than what God had given me. But as I grow in understanding my true ability amidst the warfare and turmoil, I humbly thank Him for the measure I've been entrusted with. I am, all at once, quite content to walk out this stretch of the journey, because goodness–what I have on my plate is enough! And so is He…*more than enough.*

I've gone through seasons as an adult where my time in God's Word has been minimal. I have so much of it memorized from childhood, after all. I've read the Bible cover to cover. What could possibly be in there that's worth me putting my phone down or getting up a little earlier? This thinking comes either from being overwhelmed with the chaos of life or thinking I have things under control, believing I don't need help. Both are rooted in a lie that keeps me from His heart.

As we spend time soaking up God's written Word we have the opportunity to surrender all we are and all we have to His sovereign control. Sovereign means that He is over it all–the ultimate Authority. And the thing about our God is that He doesn't use "control" in the same way humans do. He didn't program us with preset responses to the hard things we face, though He could have. Instead, He granted us free will in all our responses and decisions.

When we deepen our relationship with the very One who created us, we understand this critical connection we have with Him. We grasp with our finite minds that *He is life* and the fulfillment of every good thing. Opening the Bible and leaning in to know Him *anew* exposes the lies that keep me spiraling out of control, isolated from the very God and people who would infuse *life, freedom, and purpose* into the depths of my soul.

We haven't even come close to knowing the fullness of who He is and who He created us to be, but we can lean in to know more and more of our created purpose–all the way until we're called home to glory. *So, why in the world wouldn't we?!!*

We live in a time when our Christian freedoms are by and large protected here in the United States of America. For this, we should be profoundly grateful. But historically, persecution has grown the church and kept us desperate for Him. Apathy grows wild where we grow comfortable. Jennie Allen says, *"We get stuck because we believe God to be a God we go to church for, but not a God we risk our lives for."* This belief isn't Biblical salvation.

Darkness is taking ground right in front of us, yet we can't imagine being pulled from our modern comforts to confront evil with His truth and light. I say this with so much humility because, apart from remembering my lowest points, I too leisurely stroll through my days, picking and choosing the level at which I participate in the spiritual battle around me. *Salvation is surrender, and it costs us greatly.*

When we have face-to-face communion with our Savior, we cannot help but surrender our comforts and join in the battle against all that opposes true freedom, which is found in Christ alone.

Do you believe that He is more powerful than the evil around you–more powerful than your own sin? This is where true victory lies: a faith built on the truth of who He is, giving meaning and purpose to who you were created to be. *Ask Him to show you who He is*. I ask Him this often. I have to ask again and again, because I get comfortable and I forget. My faith becomes about practices and niceties instead of stemming from a place of knowing who God really is in my midst.

This constant remembrance and building upon what I previously knew about Him changes everything. Pause for some self-evaluation: Are you walking in dependence or independence with your Savior? Draw near to Him, and He will help you walk in victory and freedom–and then, through the way you live your life and share your story, offer that freedom to others.

"But He gives more grace. Therefore it says, 'God opposes the proud but gives grace to the humble.' Submit yourselves therefore to God. Resist the devil, and he will flee from you. Draw near to God, and

He will draw near to you. Cleanse your hands, you sinners, and purify your hearts, you double-minded." –James 4:6-8

Below is how the Holy Spirit illumined my mind (supernaturally opened my eyes) to His truth as I read His Word this morning. This is how He leads me to apply His truth directly to my life in real time.

> **[PSALM 96]**
> **Worship in the Splendor of Holiness**
>
> **Oh sing to the Lord a new song;**
> **sing to the Lord, all the earth!**
> **Sing to the Lord, bless His name;**
> **tell of His salvation from day to day.**
> **Declare His glory among the nations,**
> **His marvelous works among all the peoples!**

I won't borrow from yesterday's work. I will lean in to know of Your power anew today, Jesus, and from this place, I will invite others in. Open my eyes to the opportunities You bring my way to share Your salvation today. Keep me close to those things in my life that serve to remind me You are my Savior, so the Gospel of truth continues to fuel my hope.

> **For great is the Lord, and greatly to be praised;**
> **He is to be feared above all gods.**
> **For all the gods of the peoples are worthless idols,**

but the Lord made the heavens.
Splendor and majesty are before Him;
strength and beauty are in His sanctuary.

You alone are worth my adoration and praise, Jesus! Keep my heart pure for You and my eyes open to see Your work before me in all of creation. Still my heart again to know of Your strength and beauty through the birds singing, the flowers blooming, the sun shining, and the breeze blowing. Your presence is my sanctuary.

Ascribe to the Lord, O families of the peoples,
ascribe to the Lord glory and strength!
Ascribe to the Lord the glory due His name;
bring an offering, and come into His courts!

In Your strength, use me to cultivate worship of You within my home and everywhere You lead me. Take all I have as a humble offering, and use it for Your glory alone, Jesus.

Worship the Lord in the splendor of holiness;
tremble before Him, all the earth!
Say among the nations, "The Lord reigns!
Yes, the world is established; it shall never be moved;
He will judge the peoples with equity."

Because You are set apart and not confined by the brokenness of this world, lead me by Your gracious hand to fear You above all else. You reign, Lord

Jesus! You have established the very world I live in, so I can trust that nothing will happen apart from Your sovereign will. You are a good God, and Your judgment is perfect. Wrongs will indeed be righted, and justice is Yours! I may not see it today, but my hope finds its resting place in You because I know You will make it all right one day.

> **Let the heavens be glad, and let the earth rejoice;**
> **let the sea roar, and all that fills it;**
> **Let the field exult, and everything in it!**
> **Then shall all the trees of the forest sing for joy**
> **before the Lord, for He comes,**
> **for He comes to judge the earth.**
> **He will judge the world in righteousness,**
> **and the peoples in His faithfulness.**

All of creation worships You, Jesus! And so will I! Cause the troubles on my mind to give way to the evidence of Your mercy and grace that surrounds me. You are only ever just, and Your way is faithful and true. Help me follow Your gentle promptings throughout the day as I reconcile these truths with my current reality. Change everything I thought I knew, bringing it into submission to the new work You would do in my midst through my surrender. Amen.

Will you come into His presence seeking?

When you're walking in dependence on your Savior, you will walk in victory–over fear, over anger…over sin. We cannot offer that freedom to others if we are in bondage to something. Although the topic I share next is a hard one, please invite the Holy Spirit in as you read. Let's be discerning and not dismissive–leaving no stone unturned that may be hiding sin in our hearts and lives.

Pornography and Sex Trafficking

In the church, pornography has long been on the blacklist because it is seen as a man or woman failing to keep their heart pure. *"If a man but thinks of a woman with lust in his heart he has committed adultery."* This is true. The church has done well to bring to light how pornography destroys marriages and families. It is a gateway drug to other sexual sins, as it only satisfies in the moment for a season, and then the user inevitably dives deeper into the depravity–looking to escort services, homosexuality, prostitution, and pedophilia to satisfy their corrupt, lustful desires.

Here's where the church as a whole has neglected to fully comprehend or bring to light: *pornography is a huge part of sex trafficking*. Pornography creates the demand for women and children to be supplied for sexual use–many of whom are trafficked to fill that demand. And while there is no possible way of knowing who is and who isn't being trafficked on the deep dark web, the pornographic consumer must reconcile their conscience with the fact that their choice to engage in pornography affects far more than just themselves or their families.

Whether or not an individual on the other side of the screen is being trafficked is not the tip of the spear that would shred any argument defending pornography, though it is a strong one. The deeper truth is this: as a pornographic consumer, you are placing yourself in the role of a Pimp or a John. You have made the choice, over and over again, to degrade the person in front of you–someone made in the image of God–reducing them to a mere product to be exploited. As the church, we need to have real conversations about how devious and demonic pornography truly is.

For those addicted to pornography, I extend grace to you. This connection may have never occurred to you. There is help. There is forgiveness. There is grace. There is hope. There is freedom. But committing, here and now, to radically uproot this addiction and get help is a non-negotiable. *Covenant Eyes, Bark, and Canopy* are all online filters created for protection and accountability. You cannot fight darkness while remaining hidden in it. You must bring it into the light and get help. As always, Jesus knows the way.

Did you know that the top three porn sites in the world receive a combined 134,491 new website visits *per minute*? And that most pornographic videos contain some depiction of aggression and violence? Did you also know that most young people are exposed to pornography by the time they are 11-13 years old? Research has shown pornography consumption is frequent. One study from 2020 found that, among 18- to 73-year-olds, 91.5% of men and 60.2% of women surveyed reported having consumed pornography within the past month.[1]

These statistics reveal that people's minds are being influenced by the reality of pornography and the violence it often depicts. Research is finding that users are more likely to hold erroneous sexual beliefs. According to Fight the New Drug, research shows porn consumers who engage more consistently are *"more likely to express an intent to rape, less likely to intervene during a sexual assault, more likely to victim-blame survivors of sexual assault, more likely to support violence against women, more likely to forward sexts without consent, more likely to commit actual acts of sexual violence, and ... more willing to purchase sex."*[1]

The sad reality of the modern age is that the only way to truly end sex trafficking is to cut off the demand. And that demand is fueled by the explosive and pervasive distribution and consumption of pornography, which now begins distorting the brains of boys and girls around the world at an average age of less than 10 years old.

As Fight the New Drug puts it, *"Economics 101 tells us the demand fuels the supply. And, unfortunately, the demand for younger performers is living up to that principle, simultaneously creating porn 'stars' and sex trafficking victims."* Sex trafficking and pornography are inextricably linked.

CHAPTER 14

WHERE IS HE LEADING YOU NOW

As we heal, our sensitivity to the Lord's leading in our lives grows stronger. When we spend time with Him, we learn to know His voice apart from the voice of the masses. We are in the best place possible to *"walk by faith and not by sight."* So *lean into* His promptings. Remember, you are a new creation in Jesus. You ought to look, speak, and act differently than others–or even than you might expect from yourself. It can feel intimidating to put yourself out there as you take steps of faith in obedience to His calling, but one thing is for certain: as you step out, you can expect Him to show up and do what only He can do.

If you don't have a sweet pocket of brothers and sisters in Christ that are a safe space–leaning in together with you to know His heart on your behalf (and you leaning in to know His heart on their behalf)–then pray for it. You were not made to walk this out alone. Jesus doesn't just call us to impossible things; *He equips us to do impossible things*. And He surrounds us with the rest of His body to complement the work He is doing within us.

In seasons where Chris and I haven't had deep community, Jesus has consistently asked us to lead from a place of vulnerability and create this space for others. *And why wouldn't He call us to the work of multiplying what He began in us?* Even in the beginning, Adam and Eve communed with God long before there were other human beings around. He was enough for them when things were perfect, and when they were deceived and fell away, their communion with Him was restored because He made for them a covering and future promise of redemption because of their sins. He is enough for us now as we grapple with what we're pursuing that keeps us enslaved–and He is there for us again when we choose to surrender it, and again when we walk in freedom and invite others to do the same. He has always and ever will be *enough*.

A contrite spirit, a humble heart, and a life surrendered are evidence of God's redemptive power at work through our brokenness. It's the most compelling testimony we could offer a hurting world. It's a posture of deliverance, healing, hope, and power–a life lived in such a way that darkness is exposed and His light shines through words seasoned with compassion and actions rooted in unconditional love.

One-on-one discipleship identifies the contradiction between our confessional theology and our functional theology.[1] Because we are human, we have blind spots. We also need encouragement, perspective, and others to bear up under burdens too heavy for us to carry alone. Intentionality is required to cultivate space for meaningful relationships, built upon the framework that is Christ Jesus. Inviting believers who are further along in their journeys to speak life into us is one of the ways God pours His grace out on us. Invite it! *We all need corrective and protective relationships.*

Don't overcomplicate it, just grab a brother or sister in Christ and start talking about Jesus! Jesus grabbed twelve guys and He was intentional with them. They ate together, prayed together, lived together…and then He left the mission to us.

"You don't have to have a head for it, you just need to have a heart for it. The great commission is this: because you have been with Me, go be with people, so that they can be with Me."

–Jennie Allen

We know what it looks like to be with Jesus because we have the Gospels. From there, we can commit to figuring it out together with other believers. Learn together who you are in Christ (your identity and worth), know His truth (understand the Bible), and give away God (share with others). Allow me to help you get started.

In Christ I am:

- Courageous (Deuteronomy 31:6)
- Accepted (Romans 15:7)
- Rescued (Colossians 1:13-14)

- A child of God (John 1:12)
- An heir together with Jesus (Romans 8:17)
- Never Alone (Joshua 1:9)
- Valuable (Luke 12:6-7)
- A work in Progress (Philippians 1:6)
- Chosen (Colossians 3:12)
- Loved (John 3:16)
- A New Creation (2 Corinthians 5:17)
- Free (Galatians 5:1)
- Filled with Purpose (Jeremiah 29:11)
- Treasured (Deuteronomy 14:2)
- Precious (Isaiah 43:4)
- Wonderfully Made (Psalm 139:14)
- Enough (2 Corinthians 12:9-10)
- God's Masterpiece (Ephesians 2:10)

God is:

- Creator (Genesis 1:1)
- Eternal (Psalm 90:2)
- Present (Hebrews 13:5)
- Immutable (James 1:7) –He is unchanging
- Self-sufficient (Exodus 3:14)
- Omniscient (Psalm 139:1) –He knows all things
- Sovereign (Ephesians 1:11)–He directs it all
- Holy (Leviticus 19; Isaiah 6:3)
- Jealous (Exodus 34:14) –He wants me for His own
- Gracious (Ephesians 2:4)
- Wise (1 Corinthians 1:20-26)
- Omnipotent (Jeremiah 32:17) –All-powerful
- Patient (2 Peter 3:9)

- Good (Psalm 86:5)
- Righteous (Romans 2:6)
- Faithful (2 Timothy 2:13)
- Truth (Numbers 23:19; John 16:13)
- Infinite (Psalm 147:5)
- Peace (2 Thessalonians 3:16)
- Hope (Psalm 71:5)
- Everlasting Father (Isaiah 9:6)
- Sustainer (Psalm 54:4; Deuteronomy 32:6)
- Eternal Life (1 John 5:20)
- Love (1 John 1:9)
- Just (Deuteronomy 32:4; Psalm 25:9)
- Shelter (Joel 3:16)
- Listener (1 John 5:14)
- Hiding Place (Psalm 32:7)
- Advocate (1 John 2:1)
- Healer (Exodus 15:26; Malachi 4:2)
- Perfecter (Hebrews 12:2)
- Refuge from the Storm (Isaiah 25:4)
- Trustworthy (Psalm 56:3; 145:13)
- Restorer (Psalm 23:3)
- Everlasting Light (Isaiah 60:20)
- Compassionate (Psalm 147:3; Lamentations 3:22)
- Gracious (Isaiah 30:18; Hebrews 4:16)
- Purifier (Malachi 3:3)
- Refiner (Malachi 3:2-3)
- Strength (Psalm 43:2)
- Bread of Life (John 6:35)
- Resting Place (Jeremiah 50:6)
- Provider (Genesis 22:14)
- Living Water (John 4:10)

- Helper (Hebrews 13:6)
- Shield (Psalm 144:2)
- Mediator (1 Timothy 2:5-6)
- Stronghold in the Day of Trouble (Nahum 1:7)
- Comfort (Romans 15:5)
- Friend (John 15:15)
- Fortress (Psalm 18:2)
- Wonderful Counselor (Isaiah 9:6; Psalm 16:7)
- Deliverer (Psalm 70:5)
- Author of my Faith (Hebrews 12:2)
- Savior (1 John 4:10; Isaiah 12:2; Isaiah 45:22)
- Resurrection (John 11:25)
- Overcomer (John 16:33)
- Redeemer (Isaiah 59:20)

"An infinite God can give all of Himself to each of His children. He does not distribute Himself that each may have a part, but to each one He gives all of Himself as fully as if there were no others."

–A.W. Tozer

You don't need anything more than what you have. A disciple of Jesus is someone who is following Jesus, being changed by Jesus, and is committed to the mission of Jesus.

When I was only six years old, there was a faithful older woman who taught my Sunday school class. I specifically remember her gentleness. She committed to creating a space for us to know Jesus week after week. It was there, in her class, that the Spirit of God moved me to repent of my sins, accept Jesus' free gift of salvation, and enter into a personal relationship with Jesus.

A few years later, another older woman energetically acted out each and every biblical account she shared with us. She did this weekly and she did it with such passion that children of all ages leaned in with all we had, eager to know the God of the Bible more deeply. "Grandma Johnson" became family–and a safe space for us all.

During that same time, we had a pastor who did life with my dad. It changed our family dynamic entirely. He offered so much more than mere words; he met us in our suffering and walked it out with us. I was too young to grasp much of the discipleship piece until this same pastor and his sweet wife, seeing the heartache in the local public school system, were moved with compassion. They opened up their hearts and home to seven of us (plus their three children) and started a private school. It was an old-fashioned, one-room schoolhouse of sorts. We became part of their family as we gathered around their table, and they poured Jesus into us daily.

Then, in high school, there was another pastor's wife who was simply authentic. She loved Jesus unapologetically and had a laugh that could light up an entire room. I immediately sensed, after meeting her for the first time, that I could talk to her about anything, as did others. She was approachable and held my current reality with compassion and grace.

She lived her life in such a way that it felt like an open invitation. Her tone was never harsh, and her words were never condemning. Jesus beautifully made space for others through her humble, surrendered heart, and He still does today.

God was also making space for me through a couple of friends from public school during my incredibly difficult season of abuse. They didn't know the fullness of what was happening, but during our freshman year, they always made time for me. Whether it was a quick exchange of words in passing between classes, a hug after school, or doing life together in the years that followed…they were genuine friends who loved me for me–not for what I could give them. Life on life with them was a welcome reprieve from the inner turmoil I was desperately trying to escape. Although our face-to-face connections are seldom these days, our hearts remain close through periodic texts and phone calls.

In Bible college, I discovered mutual accountability and discipleship through a group of girls who came alongside and loved me forward. When I swayed from what they discerned was God's best for me, they continued eating meals with me, studying with me, and praying for me. A couple of them especially leaned in to learn God's heart for me along the way. They were the first to celebrate God's work in my life as I discovered who I was in Him. I had sweet sisterhood on the journey. Although we are now spread around the world, these women remain a tender source of encouragement in my spiritual journey, ever eager to lean in and know His heart for me in each season.

Throughout our twenty years in ministry, many have willingly made space for Chris, the kids and me. They weren't the ones with a list full of expectations; they've been tender in their words, consistent in their encouragement, and humble in their counsel. They've filled the role of grandparents and parents, imparting their sage wisdom into the spaces we've shared. They've been peers, shouldering the weight of ministry with us, and comrades in the battle. Some have even been young enough to be our children, yet they eagerly invite us into the tangible ways Jesus is showing up through their bold questions as they settle for nothing less than an authentic God who still works miracles.

Are you the pastor, pastor's wife, grandparent, or friend? Are you the peer or parent? There is a place for you!! We need you! *The body of Christ is not operating at its fullest potential until you engage.* Remember, it's a humble spirit and contrite heart that God desires, so seek Him above all. Before you commit to another, commit to your relationship with Him, and discipleship will naturally happen. He will do it through you.

"And Jesus came and said to them, 'All authority in heaven and on earth has been given to me. Go therefore and make disciples of all nations, baptizing them in the name of the Father and of the Son and of the Holy Spirit, teaching them to observe all that I have commanded you. And behold, I am with you always, to the end of the age.'"
–Matthew 28:18-20

"Discipleship is profoundly more than a set of strategies. Discipleship is profoundly more than workable systems. Discipleship is about transformation of the heart. Without the transformation of the heart, without a focus on the heart of every disciple of Jesus Christ, nothing will produce what you're seeking to produce."

–Paul David Tripp

CHAPTER 15

GLORY TO GLORY

In His presence, obedience is the most natural response to His calling. His glory shifts and changes how we see life itself. It changes how we suffer and surrender. *Glory* is defined as the manifest presence of Jesus–*Jesus made real* in your life and mine. *Glory to glory* refers to a progressive journey from one degree of glory to another. It's an ever-increasing glory. The longer we journey with Him, the more we can see that He is walking with us, and others can see it too.

I struggle saying no to people. By God's grace, I am still alive to write these words to you. In too many instances–mostly in my teen years–my actual life was in danger. When I was 14, I was so desperate to fit in and be accepted that instead of exercising caution with a new friend, I made certain not to miss out on a sleepover. Then, when an older guy asked me to leave her house with him, I decided not to risk losing the only man I believed thought I was beautiful. I abandoned all reason in following him out the door. To where? To do what? I didn't know. It's not that these questions weren't ruminating within me, I just didn't want this guy to think I questioned his character. And this was *after* he told me his rap sheet of crimes and parole status. He warranted his character being called into question! But my deep desire for acceptance blinded me to the danger. I assumed the risk instead of making this stranger I didn't know work for my trust.

If I'm honest, I'm kind of in freak-out mode right now. *Jesus, I know You are here with me...please keep proving it*! I have two weeks before I need to send this book off to the publisher. It's not the writing that has me freaking out–it's the fact that, up until now, it's just been Jesus and me working through the darkest, hardest moments of my story on these pages. It's become such beautiful, sacred ground for me. But it's incredibly vulnerable. The thought of it going out to the general public is terrifying because it's so different from sharing it within the context of my beloved small group or one-on-one with a dear sister in Christ. There will be no back-and-forth discussion. I'm not guaranteed that my words will rest on your heart and spur you on in your own healing journey as I intend them to. And yet, if I'm honest, I crave your acceptance. Your approval. I can't fathom harsh criticism of my most vulnerable inner healing spaces.

I am a work in progress. I deeply desired to write this book from the tone of "join me as I continue to journey" rather than "I have it all figured out". It's in the struggle to surrender how this book will be received that Jesus is meeting me. It's a call to relinquish control over things I don't really have control over but *feel* like I need to control over for the assurance that it's all gonna be okay.

I thought, after all these years of surrender and allowing Jesus to use my story for His purposes, that I had learned not to be so much of a people-pleaser. But even now, when my mind and body begin to feel uneasy, instead of pausing to know God's wisdom in the moment, I often default to making the other person feel at ease. It's a pattern I am wholly dependent on Jesus to reset–people-pleasing, even with strangers. At 42 years old, I am grateful to finally see that this problem has kept me from knowing more fully His peace and rest. My progression from glory to glory is that Jesus is helping me recognize when I am seeking another's approval and acceptance over His and to know, on an ever-deepening level, my inherent value as His beloved daughter.

As I pray through these last few chapters, I'm asking Jesus to reveal which parts of my story to share next. In looking back and recognizing His presence, even when I couldn't feel it at the time, He is bringing so much peace and rest as my heart is tempted to be afraid of what's to come. I remember similar feelings from long ago–a complete vulnerability and inability to protect myself.

A couple of years ago, it was a step of shaky faith that landed me on the phone with the young woman who worked with sex trafficking survivors. God used that *simple offering of obedience* to open my eyes to the reality of His work when I needed Him most. Because of that step, I was able to somewhat absorb the reality that I was nearly enslaved into sex trafficking myself–a reality that, if it had come to fruition, would have massively changed my life. No more warm bed to curl up in each night. No more predictable Monday-Friday schedule with easy weekends. No more going row by row in church to hug everyone or baking sugar cookies and pumpkin bread with my mom and sisters over the holidays. No more stopping to soak in the smell of rain as it hit the desert sand. No more birthday celebrations or simple trips to the grocery store. No more freedom. No more autonomy. No more peace. No more dreaming. No more becoming. No more love. Only bondage and constant, perpetual horror.

I have a lump in my throat and tears in my eyes as I write these words. Profound humility and awe swell within my soul because that never became my reality. I am acutely aware that God protected me when I was most vulnerable and couldn't protect myself. The very faith journey He began in me threatened to expose the darkness, and so my abusers let me go. There was a spiritual battle waging war over my future greater than I could've known, but God said, "Here is where it stops, Satan. I have other plans for Crystal's life." *And Satan had to obey.* Because God is greater–greater than anything and everything that comes against us. I couldn't see it at fourteen, but now, as I come to know Jesus more intimately, I'm compelled to take these shaky steps of faith toward what He's calling me to. In this sacred, fully dependent place, I can now retrospectively see the evidence of His presence in my life when I thought it was all falling apart.

Brothers and sisters, it is the very presence of God that we reflect to a hurting world through our broken stories. It's *His glory* being revealed. As we walk with Him, we see His presence more plainly and share more readily with others the reason for the hope we have. *Glory to glory* is a journey of transformation from one degree of glory to another. Together, as we each reflect God's glory, we contribute to a greater revelation of His nature to a hurting world.

Just as Jesus provided physical protection in my most vulnerable state by not allowing me to be trafficked, He tenderly reminds me now that I don't have to know how publishing a book containing my darkest, most intimate moments to an unknown audience will unfold. I only need to lean into the reality that He is right here with me–the same God He has always been–advocating for me and protecting me from the warfare to come as my story wages war on darkness itself. He beckons you and anyone who reads these words to step into His glorious light, because there is more FREEDOM and GRACE and HOPE and HEALING than you currently know! And *it's worth* you taking a shaky step of faith. *It's worth* facing every single fear that has held you back from being who you were created to be. Jesus is calling you to redemption, and He won't stop fighting for you until all of you is bought back from the slave block.

If you've gotten this far into the book and are feeling like your life has been pretty uneventful compared to mine, please hear this: *you do not need a traumatic story for His glory to be made known in your life.* Don't for one second believe the lie that your story is less impactful because it's not like someone else's. The fact is, although none of us have the same story, we serve the same amazing God who is proving His nearness through both everyday events and life-altering ones.

How is He proving that He's real in *your* life? Your answer to this is what mankind sits on the edge of their seats for–*tangible evidence* to trust God and believe in Him. Evidence that He's worth living for and dying for. Do you know Him this intimately through the details of *your story* yet?

My youngest currently loves the Bible account of Moses and the burning bush in Exodus 34:29-35. Just last week, she was just telling me how Moses talked to God in the bush, and afterward, his face looked different. He radiated God's glory. Everyone knew Moses had been with Jesus.

My daughter's excited recounting of this story was a timely reminder. I have often feel inadequate to teach a Bible lesson, homeschool my kids, lead small group, share my heart on social media, comfort a friend deeply grieving, or write a book. The inadequacy stems from looking at my broken self myself and thinking, *"How are you going to help others apply Biblical truths that hold the power to set them free?"* The irony is, when it's Jesus I want to give, it has nothing to do with me. All I simply need to do is ask Him to open my spiritual eyes to how He is there in my midst. You see, when we've experienced Jesus, it's just plain evident to everyone around us. His glory shines brightly through us when we're caught up in His presence. And of course, He redeems the past and turns it into another tool for His Kingdom work.

In Moses' story, his face shone so brightly that he had to wear a veil or else others were afraid to come near him. God's glory–His presence–is so powerful that it consumes us. The difference for us today is that since Moses' time, God was made flesh and dwelt among us. In 2 Corinthians 3:18, Paul says that Christians, unlike Moses, do not need a veil over their faces. We can "contemplate" or "behold" the glory of the Lord with "unveiled faces." The transformative power comes from the Spirit of the Lord–as we experience Him, we are transformed into His likeness. Others will know He's real to us by our countenance, words, actions, and responses to life's difficulties.

"And we all, with unveiled face, beholding the glory of the Lord, are being transformed into the same image from one degree of glory to another. For this comes from the Lord who is the Spirit." —2 Corinthians 3:18

The "veil" Paul refers to isn't just a physical barrier but a spiritual one. He's referring to anything that hinders our vision of God and His glory. For the Israelites, it was the old covenant–a shadow of the good things to come. For us, it could be our past, our sins, our doubts, or our fears.

In Christ, this veil is taken away, and we stand face-to-face with the reality of God's grace. As we "contemplate," or focus, on the Lord's glory, a miraculous exchange happens: we are being transformed into His image. The source of this transformative power is the Spirit of God who dwells in us. He reminds us that we are not alone on the journey. The Holy Spirit is constantly at work in us, enabling us to overcome the veils that once blinded us and shaping us to be more like Christ.[1]

What veils might be hindering you from seeing God's glory? Is it a commitment to self-reliance, a habit of sin, a fear of the unknown? Draw near to God through His Word and by simply talking to Him. Invite Him into your real-life struggles. And you already know how passionate I am about having a handful of brothers and sisters who see you living your life and have permission to speak into it regularly–to encourage, confront, support, hold accountable, walk with you, and love you toward Jesus' heart. As we experience God in these ways, we can expect the transformative work of the Spirit to take place in our lives.

Because of Jesus, we have direct access to God 24/7. We can boldly approach the throne of grace with confidence so that we can receive mercy and grace to help us in our time of need (Hebrews 4:16). This direct access holds the potential to radically change us and how others witness His presence in our lives. But are we actually leaning into that potential? There is no place where the power of His presence in our lives is more intimately known than in our very own homes.

Home is our most intimate space. Home is where our truest, most authentic self is known. We can't fake anything for long with those we do life with day in and day out. God uses home and family as a powerful space for His most authentic work in us. But sometimes, we get caught up in the false belief that our greatest work lies outside of our four walls. There are plenty of serving opportunities found in church, the workplace, and the community. The enemy loves when we take the bait, using up our giftedness and pouring out all our energies on everyone and everything except on those within our home. Satan fears the power that would work in the midst of our homes unlike any other transformation power.

The family unit was established by God in creation, set apart for Kingdom purpose. It's no wonder the Biblical model of family is under such attack today. Within the home, we get a front row seat to the real-time work God is doing in each other's lives. Years of relational investment surrendered for God's Kingdom purposes form a powerful assault on the weapons that come against us. In the home, we experience the privilege of intimate proximity with other human beings also created in the image of God. When we steward these shared spaces–from a heart level to the physical constructs of the home–God's work is astronomically multiplied.

When God does a transformative work within us, our families receive the precious first fruits of that transformation power, which will impact not only our children but our children's children and their children. Generational sins and strongholds are brought to light, challenged, surrendered, and broken. Why we do what we do as a family is rooted in an ever-deepening understanding of our created purpose. We are constantly present to cheer one another on in the good and hold one another in the bad. Selfishness, pride, envy, and anger…it's all laid bare in the home. It's a blessing that the fruit of the flesh has nowhere to hide! When we are walking in darkness, those who live with us are usually the first to know.

It takes a whole lot of Holy Spirit power, but when we respond biblically to each other's sins, it's an accurate and compelling representation of God's unconditional love–far more accurate than a response from someone who has never seen us at our worst, someone who only knows the parts of us that we've presented to them.

There is also the crucial role the family plays in spiritual warfare. Pastor Tyler Staton from Bridgeton Church in Portland, Oregon, says there are two ways God wins against the enemy: through removal and through redemption. We need to ask God if He wants to remove the suffering we're experiencing or redeem it by depositing in us aspects of His character and Kingdom that we would never trade, even if we could choose to avoid the suffering. If He chooses to redeem it, submission is the way we receive rest, peace, and comfort. The people closest to us can become agents in manifesting the character of God in our lives, helping us persevere.

There is no one in the world I'd rather suffer alongside than my sweet husband and kids. Radical love pours out of them when the Spirit moves them on my behalf. It is the privilege of my life to stand in the gap between what my family knows and what He would reveal to them, advocating for them in prayer and serving them daily. With family, no one carries the load alone. We all join in and share the burden. Even our precious kids are learning how they've been uniquely gifted to play an integral role in meeting the needs of others.

God uses home as a sacred place where we cultivate unconditional love, joy, peace, patience, kindness, goodness, faithfulness, gentleness, and self-control. *The fruit of the Spirit becomes tangible within the family of God as we suffer together.*

As I write, I soberly recall a time the enemy caused me to lose sight of the beauty of the home and the real-time work Jesus was doing there. As a newly pregnant Mama, my heart desired nothing more than to stay home after the birth of our child. At the time, I was working part-time as an administrative assistant for a church–a job I loved, surrounded by people I loved. Circumstances changed at the church, and I was warmly welcomed into another Christian office. It was a beautiful and gracious work opportunity for the season of life I was in. Just months into this new position, I gave birth to our firstborn. Maternity leave was up in the blink of an eye, and I mourned leaving my child to go back to work. I cried often, desperate to be home, to be there around the clock, nurturing and loving my family. It was a deep desire that kept me at the feet of Jesus, pleading for Him to make a way.

Then, one day, He provided for me to be home with our children (we had two by this time). To make it work financially, I provided daycare for our sweet neighbors. Within a year, along came our baby girl through adoption. We were living the dream–our family of five, plus two additional sweet little souls, Monday through Friday. After two years of being a daycare provider, we took a step of faith and began living frugally off one income. I was passionate about not giving up the front-row seat to my children's learning and development, so we decided I would homeschool them. I was doing it–something I felt called to deep down in my soul.

But then the lie crept in.

With Chris being a pastor, there were so many amazing opportunities to have other women and young ladies over to our house for discipleship and mutual encouragement. In 2014, I found myself on the cusp of figuring out who God was in my story, and I eagerly filled up my discretionary time with intentional connections outside my family. And that's when it happened. Somewhere in those early months of finally being able to stay home full-time with my babies, my heart strings were being pulled elsewhere.

I could be more effective for God if I didn't have to spend so much time here at home.

My kids are...in the way of what God is calling me to do.

It's all-out war in the enemy's camp to keep us from becoming all we were created to be, so that we miss our chance to call out and equip our children to become everything they are created to be. The enemy knew the potential healing and redemptive power that would fill our home–and then extend far beyond its walls–if we fully embraced the unique roles we play within our family unit.

Thankfully, no sooner than the sentiments above formed into words in my mind, they were exposed. I knew for certain this was not God's voice. I was *called to cultivate home* as a place for my family to know and be known, to love them toward Jesus as I filled up with Him and poured Him out day and night.

What I am not saying here is that it's wrong for a mother to work outside the home. It does make intentional discipleship of your children more complicated, as you have less capacity to do so. But you must seek His heart in your circumstances to know whether you have bought into the lie that your worth is greater outside the home, or if you are genuinely where you're supposed to be. I wish we were having a cup of coffee on my couch so we could talk and pray through your specific situation, because I would love nothing more than to encourage you toward His heart right where you are!

Also, for my single friends, Jesus 100% wants your home to be sacred ground where His glory is known by you first, and then by all who enter. Soak in Jesus in your most intimate spaces, and watch in awe as He pours out into all aspects of your life!

The truth I needed to embrace was that our children are not in the way of who God created us to be. We have been granted stewardship over their hearts, minds, and souls for just a short time. Parenthood is a fight to sow intentional seeds into the next generation and not give in to the weariness that threatens to overwhelm and overtake us. The enemy will do everything to convince us that cultivating home is the lesser good. Don't buy into it, brothers and sisters!

There's also the temptation to cultivate the *appearance* that our homes are beautiful, restful spaces. Hospitality is a spiritual gift Chris and I share, butI learned over the years how draining it was to invite people into the *appearance* of a put-together home versus the reality of us, and our home, being a work in progress. Turns out, snapping orders at my family just moments before company arrived, as I did some last-minute rage cleaning, only cultivated a spirit of frustration as I went hard after the image of perfection. And kids are quick to call that mess out, too!

"You always want the house to look perfect when people come over!"

"I hate when we have people over because we have to clean everything!"

Yes, these words were spoken by my precious children on several occasions, and finally, I heard them. I finally sensed deeply how I was grieving the Spirit of God by dragging my kids into the burden of presenting a perfectly clean and tidy home to others. It's not relatable, and it only invites others to strive for that same put-together appearance.

When Jesus becomes real in our hearts, it changes how we live within the walls of our homes. And when we invite others in, they will feel the evidence of Jesus' transformation power at work and be compelled to lean in and know it for themselves. You cannot manufacture intimate spaces where God's work is being done. We simply must surrender, and He does the work.

One of the most powerful weapons against the darkness is when we cultivate spiritual gifts, safety, bravery, rest, healing, and redemption–*and then invite others in.* May all we do be an overflow of who we genuinely are in our most intimate of spaces.

How You Can Help End Sex Trafficking

You can make that better world a reality. You can help end sex trafficking by simply refusing to participate in the production, distribution, or consumption of pornography.

You can teach your kids about the internet–about its dangers, and about the great worth we ALL have as human beings. You can refuse to partake in seemingly harmless Youtube videos where people laugh at someone else's misfortune. The disconnect between one person's humanity and ours in a video is enough to slowly persuade us that these aren't real people, and what's being done to them isn't that harmful–either to them *or* to us.

Kids need adults to show them what healthy relationships and human interactions look like–*and what they don't look like.*

One child at a time, it's up to us to show the next generation how much suffering that behavior causes, and why we should strive to prevent it.[2]

PART 6

REDEEM BROKENNESS

CHAPTER 16

HOW CAN I GIVE BACK WITH THIS HEALING

Our purpose should never ever be tied up in what we can *do* for God and others, but rather in who we are in Him, secured in the reality of who He is. Meeting the needs of others isn't evil, but the devil likes to cross wires at this junction of our redemptive journey–getting us to do the right things for the wrong reasons. If we show up with a heart that's desperate for affirmation and validation, we'll inevitably be working as unto men, not as unto the Lord. We become enslaved by others' responses, or lack thereof, in our service.

"Emotional and spiritual maturity cannot be separated."

–Jennie Allen

The only possible way we can live as an open invitation for others to heal and walk in freedom with us is to remain connected to our Father–that when His Spirit moves, we move. We must remain dependent on the only One who is worthy. Uncomfortable circumstances can keep us in sweet dependency on Him. Our greatest potential to effect change around us is to first be changed ourselves. It's His work in us that allows transformative work to take place through us into the hearts and lives of others.

Commit to your healing journey. Allow Jesus to lead you into the uncharted waters of your past, present, and future. He knows the way–all we have to do is follow.

But let's be real…there are things that completely stop us in our tracks and keep us from taking another step. I experienced this last fall when I was leaning in to know why God had me create space to hear His voice. I was not posting on social media or mindlessly doing anything other than intentionally waiting for Him to move. I could sense He was calling me to something so much bigger than myself. That *holy discontentment* kept me leaning in, eager to know what was next. I was expectant, things were moving along–and then fear crept in like an evil villain, threatening to hijack my resolve to write this book.

To set the scene, I need to back up to a few weeks earlier when I had invited a friend over for early morning coffee and breakfast. We talked quietly at the kitchen counter for a long while before the rest of my family awoke. We got together to share our stories. So much hurt…so much opportunity for redemption. We recounted the ways God is buying back the hardest parts of our lives for His glory, somehow turning it all into something beautiful within us too.

After I shared my story, my dear friend said she had someone she wanted me to meet–a woman in her small group who had been trafficked in her teenage years. As soon as she said the words, my body grew tense. I began to perspire, my heart raced, and my stomach tied in knots. But I simply replied, "Oh, yes! That would be great. I should get together with her." We prayed together, hugged, and shortly after arriving back home, my friend sent me this woman's phone number.

I can tell you, everything within me did *not* want to talk with her. And there it was–something unearthed from deep within me. It had been directing my thoughts, stirring up doubt, and keeping me silent ever since I discovered in my late thirties that I had been groomed for sex trafficking. *I wasn't actually trafficked. So, who am I to associate my story with those who actually lived, or are still living, this real-life hell?* I couldn't bring myself to call her. I just couldn't share my pain without feeling like I was making a big deal over merely being groomed–somehow belittling her much harder reality in the process.

Weeks went by, and I quickly stuffed any thoughts of reaching out to her. Up until Jesus told me it was time to write this book, that is. I shared earlier what this time was like for me… "make space to hear my voice," He said. And I did. But as I waited, it felt like I was spiritually sitting on the edge of my seat, waiting with so much fear and trembling for Him to move. I knew He wanted me to start writing, but there were some specific things He wanted me to do before putting a single word to page.

One day, as I was waiting for clarity, He spoke with absolute certainty: *"Call Melody."* I didn't even have the energy to question Him. I was desperate for Him to move me forward in my healing, so I quickly sent her a text message before my fears kicked in and I changed my mind. *"Hey, Melody...this is Crystal. Our mutual friend sent me your number a while back. Would you have time to talk over the phone sometime soon?"* She quickly responded and said that the next afternoon would work. That entire evening and the following morning, I was impatient for the phone call to be over. *How was I going to start the conversation off? What if her story triggers me and sends me spiraling? What if she's offended by me sharing my story, as if I'm communicating my experiences are equally as traumatizing?* I entered the conversation with all questions and no answers–only Jesus' clear, gentle nudging to lean into it.

We introduced ourselves over the phone, and she began to share her story. With Melody's gracious permission and tender encouragement, I am humbly sharing some of it here.

She was raised in an abusive home. It was the 1970s, and her mother did what she knew to keep a roof over her and her sister's heads. But the men she brought into the home were abusive on all levels–primarily toward Melody.

She was just 14 years old when her mom, eager to get her daughters away from harm, responded to an ad in the newspaper: HELP WANTED. IN NEED OF A WOMAN TO CARE FOR MY HOME WHILE I AM AWAY ON BUSINESS. She took her girls along for the interview. As soon as Melody saw the man, she felt a sinking feeling in her stomach. But she thought of her mom who was trying to get them out of an already bad situation, so she decided not to mention a word of her uneasiness. "But my daughters will have to move in with me," her mother told the man. He assured her it would not be a problem. They agreed her mom would take the job, which seemed an incredible opportunity.

Melody silently purposed to never be in close proximity with this man. *"Should be easy,"* she thought, *"since he'll be away on business so often."* But after they moved in, the man was home nearly all the time. He had a far more sinister plan in the works than he had advertised.

The self-professed traveling businessman immediately began to groom Melody's family. Soon after, he separated Melody from her mother and sister. Then he trafficked her out for six years. She got pregnant twice during this time. He forced her to get an abortion with the first pregnancy, but she was able to keep her beautiful son. Melody was just a baby herself, but motherhood gave her a reason to keep fighting. She finally escaped, with the help of another family member and was free at last.

Sadly, because the trauma was too heavy to bear alone, many years of drug abuse and prison time followed. It was then–when she had lost everything–that she found Jesus.

Today, Melody feels a specific calling, a redemptive purpose born from her lifetime of trauma. She now provides opportunities for drug addicts to know that healing is found in a personal relationship with Jesus. "Drug addicts have trauma-filled pasts," Melody says. She knows all too well what life looks post-trauma apart from Him, so she now chooses Him daily.

Receiving her story on the other end of the phone, I sobbed. Hard. So hard that I couldn't speak. But after a few moments, words finally erupted through the tears: "I hurt so badly for you! *Why did God spare me and not you?!* I'm so sorry, Melody! I'm so sorry for all you've endured and all that you've lost. My heart is so broken for you!!" She was kind and reassuring, reminding me that she has Jesus now, and He is making it all beautiful. You guys, I know this truth. But there are some stories and experiences that test the limits of what we know to be true. Her story shattered the ceiling off what I thought possible.

But even this, Jesus? "Yes," He responded, *"even this can be redeemed."*

I attempted to recover a bit before starting into my story. Melody graciously and empathetically heard my words, and beyond. She confirmed that she also believed Uncle Mikey was the pimp in my situation. "But who am I to write a book about trafficking when *I was only groomed* to be trafficked?" I humbly asked her.

She affirmingly responded, "The grooming phase was the worst part of the whole thing…it's when they are breaking you down and trying to rebuild you into what they want you to be. I was obviously there for all the abuse after the grooming phase, but I don't remember it. The grooming was the hardest part."

It suddenly hit me, like a tidal wave carrying purpose and so much confidence in what Jesus had laid before me. He spared me from being trafficked so I could use my voice for those who have no voice. For those whose experiences have left them hopeless and alone, battered and bruised, misunderstood and rejected…I advocate for healing, for awareness of the deep darkness roaming our communities looking for its next victim, for more safe spaces to be cultivated within churches so that healing and redemption can begin for all.

Have I spiraled out of control before, triggered by something traumatic? Yep. Many times. That's

PTSD in action. Did I spiral out of control by hearing Melody's story, like I was certain I would? No, I did not. The difference was Jesus' tender leading. Talking to Melody, after His clear prompting, brought more clarity, healing, resolve–and a new, sweet sister in Christ who gets the struggle deeply. When Jesus leads us to something that feels scary, we can rest assured that He wants to use it for our personal growth and for the growth of His Kingdom. In His hands, it all becomes a tool in our sanctification journey.

It's not about being comfortable anymore, friends. The focus has shifted. With so much at stake, how can we look away and *choose* not to take that next courageous step God is calling us to? It's time to throw caution to the wind and choose faith over fear. But don't do it alone. Lean into the community He has provided for you. And if you don't have one yet, refer back to Chapter 9 and take the next step.

I think about the verse where the enemy is out to kill, steal, and destroy. But I want you to know that I really live a happy, joyous, and free life now.

"The thief (carrying out Satan's plans) comes only to steal and kill and destroy. I came that they may have life and have it abundantly."
–John 10:10

Would you pray this bravely and expectantly with me?

Jesus, give me eyes to see the brokenness in my community, and then give me the courage to move toward it as You provide clarity on next steps. Amen.

There are as many ways to respond to the hurting around us as there are people in the world. Each one of us is created to uniquely communicate His truth, love, and grace through salvation to a world that's desperate for it.

The pivotal factor is choosing to let Jesus grow you into who He made you to be–and then remaining available for the opportunities He brings your way to be that person, made in the image of God Himself.

My whole self + His redemptive work = glory unhindered + radical life change.

Eden's Glory[1] is a home that's fortifying survivors, educating communities, and working to end human trafficking all for the glory of God. And they are located just 45 minutes from my front door. Because of their specific ministry focus, I asked them to help us get a better understanding of how we can help…

How can I make space for someone to share their past trauma and encourage them on their healing journey?

- Build rapport, gain trust, and reciprocate transparency.
- Understand that trauma has an impact on the individual.
- Trauma can look like aggression, lack of focus, and avoidance.
- Behaviors, emotions, and thoughts are affected by a survivor's previous experiences: their "normal" is vastly different.
- Facilitate safety and healing by using a strength-based approach.
- View individuals through their capacities, talents, competencies, possibilities, visions, values, and hopes.
- Recognize and view problems and symptoms as adaptations to trauma.
- Offer empathy, not sympathy (don't feel sorry for them but put yourself in their shoes).
- Effective engagement consists of appropriate touch, active listening, love, boundaries, and a servant attitude.
- Recognize that many factors are at play and sole blame is not on the individual.
- Offer space and experiences that give them empowerment, voice, and choice.
- Healing begins with connection and relationship.
- Don't make promises you can't keep.

- Don't take things personally; often, if there is an issue that arises, it's related to their past trauma.
- Be patient and calm; consider your stance and your role.
- Embrace silence and its importance.
- Reaching out for help should never be more traumatizing than the event itself.
- Remember that stress hormones lead to hypervigilance and introversion.
- Let go of the idea and expectation that we should (or can) fix people.
- Each moment, day, month, or year is an opportunity to show Christ's love, safety, and community–and to help redefine hope. Don't question the impact of just one conversation.

Human trafficking is in our own backyards. Vulnerabilities are opportunities, and we can find them right in our own communities:

- Immigrants or those with limited English proficiency
- Poverty
- Natural disasters
- Family instability or family loyalty
- Runaways and Foster Children
- History of child abuse
- Insecurities or a desire for relationships
- Minors with access to the internet
- Individuals who walk to school, work, or the store alone

Since COVID, the landscape of trafficking has moved online, making any minors or young adults with apps and social media vulnerable. Familial trafficking is also on the rise due to poverty, inflation, stress, and drug use. No community is untouched. Major highways provide easy access to victims–and an easy escape.

Bringing awareness to the fact that sex trafficking is happening in our neighborhoods, and then cultivating spaces for others to heal, is part of His specific calling on my life. But there are so many opportunities to push back the darkness in your community. If trafficking isn't a burden He's placed on your heart, take this time to pray about what brokenness He is opening your eyes to.

Getting a handle on how you can help is your next point of prayer. Then take the radical steps forward–steps that run in direct opposition to how the rest of the world lives–and be Jesus to the world. Invite a brother or sister in Christ to pray alongside you over all this…invite them to shoulder the burden together with you. Then watch as Jesus multiplies the work He began in you.

"And I am sure of this, that He who began a good work in you will bring it to completion at the day of Jesus Christ." –Philippians 1:6

CHAPTER 17

HANDING OVER MY STORY FOR HIS PURPOSES

Redemption means to buy back from the slave block. We get a humble understanding of redemption in the book of Hosea. Hosea was a prophet called by God Himself to marry a woman named Gomer, who was a harlot. Why? Because God wanted their marriage and life to be a picture of His relationship with Israel. Although we don't know the specific details of Gomer's adultery, we do know that she ended up on the slave block time and time again.

I have studied this passage and do not see substantial enough evidence to indicate that Gomer was a prostitute slave or that she was being trafficked for sex, which would be a different story entirely. But she had, in some way, become indebted to others in her adulterous wanderings. This is how she ended up on the slave block. Repeatedly.

It's quite evident throughout the book that Gomer chose to have multiple sexual partners, likely for what she could gain from those relationships. Gomer obviously didn't know her inherent worth. She was clearly looking everywhere except her loving Creator to ascribe her beauty and to provide for her needs. She was desperate–but looking for help in all the wrong places. Sound familiar? All our stories highlight our need for a Savior. Here's where God shows up on the scene. Take note of His character revealed through His prophet Hosea's obedience to His calling.

Hosea, a man who spoke God's truth, spoke up above the crowd at the slave auction and bought Gomer back. He did this over and over again. He was the last person anyone would have expected to have interest in her, but he bought her back and brought her home. Hosea's love for Gomer compelled him to chase her down and redeem her from the slave block. He had compassion for her. He had patience with her. Gomer's name is Hebrew for "complete" or "fulfilled," symbolizing God's grace to all–*even the unfaithful*.

The central message of the book of Hosea is one of *redemption and restoration.* Hosea's act of love and forgiveness reflects the *unconditional love* and *redemptive grace* that God offers to all of us.

God called Hosea to chase his wife down time after time and buy her back from the actual slave block, where she stood for sale to the highest bidder. God's love for us is a love that transcends our mistakes and failures. Through Hosea, God demonstrates a love that does not fail and always welcomes us back.

"Go, show your love to your wife again... love her as the Lord loves the Israelites..."
—Hosea 3:1 NIV

We need rescue. And our only hope is a *Redeemer*.

Jesus has done for us what God told Hosea to do for Gomer. We used to be "slaves to sin" (Romans 6:17), but we have been "redeemed…with the precious blood of Christ" (1 Peter 1:18-19). He "gave Himself for us to redeem us from all wickedness and to purify for Himself a people that are His very own, eager to do what is good" (Titus 2:14). Jesus has bought us, and we belong to Him.

He bought us from the slave block for a purpose. One that is higher, greater, and far more powerful than anything we could ever dream up on our own. *And we cost Him everything*. Jesus laid down His life so that we could walk in freedom and be wholly His. That's the entire plan. That's our purpose. That our brokenness would be used as a stark backdrop to His redemptive work. Our sin–and the sins committed against us–only *highlight* His grace, power, and love in our lives.

As I've committed to letting Jesus redeem every part of my story over the years, one part lingered in the background. I knew He would lead me to walk through it one day, but I literally felt sick to my stomach at the thought of it. *Arizona itself* needed to be redeemed. It was the geographical location of my abuse, and I had no desire to return there. Although I had so many good memories of growing up in the beautiful desert and still had wonderful extended family and friends in the area, my past trauma overshadowed it all, and the thought of going back gripped me with fear and anxiety.

What if I run into one of my abusers? What about that hotel? I can't imagine driving past it. Jesus, I don't know what it looks like, but when it's time, lead me gently to accept whatever You ask me to walk through. I don't want anything or anyone to have more power over me than You do.

In 2022, we had finally accumulated enough airline miles through a credit card for five round-trip tickets to Arizona. What an incredible provision from God. It had been 12 years since Chris and I were last there–when I was pregnant with our first child. None of our kids had ever been (outside of the womb anyway) to the state where mommy was born and raised. Chris was eager to make the trip happen in December that year. It was indeed time. But I didn't want to go.

We made all the arrangements, even selecting an Airbnb in the East Valley, within fifteen minutes of where I grew up. December came, and as we packed our bags for this adventure as a family, my heart was heavy with uncertainty, as my anxiety peaked.

"Be still, and know that I am God," Jesus whispered.

We made it into our Airbnb around 1:30am. It had been a whirlwind of a travel day, and we were all exhausted. As the family settled in for the night, rest eluded me. Sleep finally came, but if it weren't for the unfamiliar, yet clean and cozy home we were in, I'm certain I wouldn't have gotten a wink. Usually, unfamiliarity feels foreign and strange. But in this moment, it was welcomed as a distraction to the familiar surroundings I was about to walk into–where so much trauma was physically housed in my past. My entire body was on high alert.

The dichotomy of feeling utterly weak, unsafe, and in imminent danger–paired with feeling altogether seen, understood, strengthened, and loved–it was completely overwhelming. It emptied me of any energy I had left. Yet, lying there in that Airbnb, I felt a deep sense of purpose and forward motion in my healing journey. It was beyond my control. Left to my own understanding, I would have never booked the flights. Being there already felt both necessary and purposeful.

The next morning, I awoke before the rest of the family and felt compelled to get in the car and drive. I told Chris I was going for coffee. I ordered my caramel almond milk latte and possibly overshared with the barista as I paid for my drink. I just couldn't hold it in. We were driving down the street to my hometown later that day, and I was bursting with fear-filled anticipation. I had one thing on my mind: coming face-to-face with what I hadn't been able to confront for 28 years. But Jesus met me with grace through that barista, and the latte was noticeably the best I had ever had.

We went grocery shopping that morning as a family because we were determined, as always, to save as much money as we could by making food ourselves on the trip. This frugal choice made our daily visits to Bahama Bucks for the best shaved ice in the entire world somehow feel non-excessive.

Every time I got into our rental car that first day, I felt deep tension. I wanted to go everywhere *but* Apache Junction, yet it was as if the SUV had a will of its own, driving me east–toward the wake of destruction still waging active war in my heart and mind. I told Chris on the way back to our Airbnb that I was tense and needed desperately to face what I had to face. And I needed to do it soon. *But what did this even mean??*

"I don't know how to functionally redeem a location, Chris! Do I just walk into the hotel? Do I pray in the lobby? Do I talk with someone behind the desk? I think...what I need to do is just drive toward the hotel and trust Jesus will guide me...but I'm physically shaking. I'm so scared."

Patiently giving me space to verbally process the vastness of what I was being called to, Chris replied, "Whatever you need to do, we are here for you." We conversed in the rawness of the moment as vulnerably as we could, with three little sets of ears in the back seat, unsure of what all the fuss was about. It was late afternoon, and we were on our way to find apparel with the Prospector logo–The Lost

Dutchman Prospector was my high school mascot and I still think it's cool.

Our first stop was Walmart on Apache Trail, just blocks from the hotel where I was raped. The closer we got, the more suffocating the oppressiveness grew in the air around me. The enemy did not want me to be freed from this geographical location. It was one of the last places where he still held my story captive, and he wasn't giving up without a fight.

As we parked the car and stepped outside, the ringing in my ears, clammy skin, and racing heart nearly overpowered me. Then, the sweet smell of rain sweeping across the desert embraced me with tender childhood memories. Rain in Arizona just hits differently. I never knew why exactly, until now–the humble creosote bush isn't much to look at, but it's responsible for the desert rain aroma. Its leaves secrete oil when dry, and after the rain, that scent is wafted into the air.[1]

Just the scent of it immediately caught me up in the presence of God. His glory was making itself known, as the beauty of life in this dry, desert terrain was ushered in through cherished memories. The smell of Arizona rain always brought me so much joyful anticipation. Desiring for my family to feel it too, I told my kids to stop and breathe it in deeply.

"It smells like a parking lot," they replied.

This little gift was obviously just for me. No one else could have possibly known how *seen* and *loved* I felt in that moment. Jesus held me there, in the tension between what He was calling me to and what He had the power to do through my obedience. He was breathing sweet life across the parched desert plains of my story. The promise of renewed life infused my heart with joy through endured suffering, filling me with anticipation of what was to come.

I am here, Jesus...I feel Your presence. I am willing. I will obey.

We searched high and low for Prospector gear and never did find any. But our adventures that week led us from one end of Apache Trail to the other, with no signs of the hotel. *Where in the world did it go?*

I'm not exactly sure when it happened, but the focal point drastically shifted from the hotel to showing my family around my hometown. We visited Goldfield Ghost Town, where we had to mine for gold, of course. We visited my brother Jim's house at the base of the iconic Superstition Mountains, where we ate a delicious home-cooked meal complete with his famous Texas toast. We stopped by my cousin Paula's Crazy Horse Saddle Shop, where she gifted us expertly crafted jewelry and glass-beaded coin purses, which she bartered with the Apache and Navajo in exchange for horse supplies. How amazing that such meaningful systems of trading goods have been preserved over the years!

We rode horses and ATVs at my cousins'. We were unexpectedly serenaded by a live Mariachi band. We drove the treacherously winding mountain roads up to Tortilla Flats, the very last stop on the old stage coach line. We ate prickly pear everything until our hearts were content. We drove past the land I grew up on, documenting all the changes since my parents sold it in 2007. We had dinner with a dear childhood friend, and were blessed as our families intermingled.

We caught up with my beloved cousins, aunts, and uncles, and even took a day trip to the gorgeous and unmatched Sedona Mountains for a quick hike amidst the red rocks, which felt like we were transported to another planet entirely. There was just so much beauty to take in–so much awe and wonder. This place I once called home was returning to me. Three long decades after I moved away, God had brought me back to the desert with my husband and children, and He made it a trip of a lifetime for us all.

Whether God blinded me from seeing the hotel or He removed it entirely, I didn't know. What I do know is that He asked me to be willing to come face-to-face with it, but He never actually led me to walk inside. My posture was ready and willing, trusting that even though I didn't understand how, He would provide. But I never did see that hotel.

A couple of weeks after returning home to the St. Louis area, I called my brother Jim. We determined to be better about keeping up with one another, and I wanted to share my story with him. We unofficially adopted Jim as a brother when I was in 8th grade. My parents helped my three sisters and me draft up a document stating that we were adopting him as our older brother, signed by each sibling. Jim was older than us and had been through severe trauma of his own, which God used to bring him into our family. As I shared my story with him and got to the part about the hotel, I asked him where it was.

"That place was bulldozed years ago, thank God," he replied.

God removed the location that gripped my heart with fear ever since the trauma. And I believe He did it just for me.

Trusting Him with every aspect of our stories is a journey–one through which He is eager to prove His worthiness of our trust. We can't possibly know what's on the other side of our obedience. But let my story compel you to take that next step of faith He is calling you to.

Get counseling. Find your community. Push back the darkness with His ever-brightening light inside. *Cultivate Redemption.*

> *"In Him we have redemption through His blood, the forgiveness of our trespasses, according to the riches of His grace, which He lavished upon us, in all wisdom and insight making known to us the mystery of His will, according to His purpose, which He set forth in Christ as a plan for the fullness of time, to unite all things in Him, things in heaven and things on earth." —Ephesians 1:7–10*

What if Jesus had chosen comfort over His purpose for coming to earth? The fact is, He chose to lean into suffering and pain because it was the Kingdom work He was meant for. His work conquered death itself on our behalf.

Our work is to point to *His* work.

If suffering is the path Jesus willingly chose, we must take a hard look at the path we choose each day. Is it the path of least discomfort? Have we journeyed so far down this path that His voice has become distant and too faint for us to notice? What would it look like to surrender all we thought we wanted in life to a God who created us for more?

Cultivation: to nurture and help grow.

Redemption: to buy back from the slave block.

Your brokenness can either *enslave you or free you*–the difference is found in surrender.

APPENDIX

Discipleship/Counseling Resources (from Ch. 8):

First, let's answer some common questions.

But don't I need a degree in counseling to counsel others?

"I myself am satisfied about you, my brothers, that you yourselves are full of goodness, filled with all knowledge and able to instruct one another." – Romans 15:14

"Let the word of Christ dwell in you richly, teaching and admonishing one another in all wisdom, singing psalms and hymns and spiritual songs, with thankfulness in your hearts to God." –Colossians 3:16

These passages (along with Ephesians 6:4, Romans 12:8, 1 Corinthians 10:11, and Titus 3:10) were written to the local church. This means everyday Joe's and Joanne's were equipped and empowered to counsel others in the early church.

What resources/tools do I need to discipleship/ counsel?

The Word of God. Do not underestimate the power of knowing He is who He says He is and sharing this powerful truth with others. You have the Holy Spirit inside, guiding you.

"All Scripture is breathed out by God and profitable for teaching, for reproof, for correction, and for training in righteousness, that the man of God may be complete, equipped for every good work." –2 Timothy 3:16-17

Is there any prep work I should do before counseling someone?

Preparation is everything if you lean into a discipleship relationship to provide clarity that leads to healing. You must rely on the help of the Holy Spirit. He will help you listen to understand, ask helpful questions to get to the heart of the matter, and discern the greatest need of the person sitting in front of you.

This means you need to spend intentional time with Jesus *regularly*. Become a man or woman of the Word, if you aren't already. Let His truths transcend your innermost being so you are free to pour this same transformative truth into others from a place of intimately knowing God. This confidence and secured hope will keep you leaning in and advocating for others. It will be a natural, seemingly effortless response to the work He has done in you.

Postures of a right heart before God:

- New Heart (Ezekiel 36:26)
- Broken and Contrite (Psalm 51:17)
- Believes in Christ Alone (Romans 10:10)
- Purified (Acts 15:9; Matthew 5:8)
- Praying (Romans 5:8; Psalm 27:8)
- Feels Conflict Within (Galatians 5:17)
- Honest, Undivided, and True (Luke 8:16; 1 Chronicles 12:33; Hebrews 10:22)

What does it actually mean to counsel another person?

There are three Hebrew words translated as "counsel" in Scripture. Together, they mean to deliberate, resolve, advise, guide, determine, purpose, consult, instruct, and plan. There are five Greek verbs for the word "counsel" which, when summarized, mean to beseech, exhort, encourage, comfort, admonish, and warn. All of these are components of Biblical counseling.

Are there times when I should defer a situation to someone with formal counseling experience?

Yes, when it becomes elevated beyond a discipleship relationship. Here are some questions to consider:

- What is the level of severity (mild, moderate, high)?

- How long has this been going on? Is it a pattern or a one-time situation?
- What kind of support system do they have? Are they using that support, or are they isolated?
- Am I the only person speaking life into them?
- What is their level of ownership? Are they repentant and grieving over their sin? Or are they just sorry they got caught?
- Did they confess and bring their sin into the light? Are they in a place of conviction or condemnation?

How you answer these questions will guide you towards either discipleship or counseling (intensive discipleship).

Okay, now that we have the stage set, *let's talk about fruit.* Just as orange trees produce oranges and apple trees produce apples, a person abiding in Christ produces the fruit of the Spirit, while one abiding in the world produces the fruit of the flesh. Sounds simple enough, right? We are going to go far beyond symptomatic approaches to healing, which alone are temporary helps at best. If we desire to reach the depths of our brokenness, we must go deeper into the heart of the behavior. This will give clarity to our next steps in healing and walking in freedom.

"Keep your heart with all vigilance, for from it flow the springs of life." –Proverbs 4:23

"The good person out of the good treasure of his heart produces good, and the evil person out of his evil treasure produces evil, for out of the abundance of the heart his mouth speaks." –Luke 6:45

"Fruit to root" is a diagnostic tool that goes beyond merely addressing behavioral problems (rearranging fruit). *Despair and fear*, for example, come from a heart of **unbelief**. Because of trauma, I personally have struggled with false beliefs about myself and God. This is part of the reason I spiraled out of control early on when revisiting past details, before I had a firm grasp on who I was and who He is. *Anger* and *foolishness* stem from a heart of **pride**. We will not dive into this at length here, but I do want to provide a basic framework that you can build upon.

Tracing the Fruit to the Root[1]

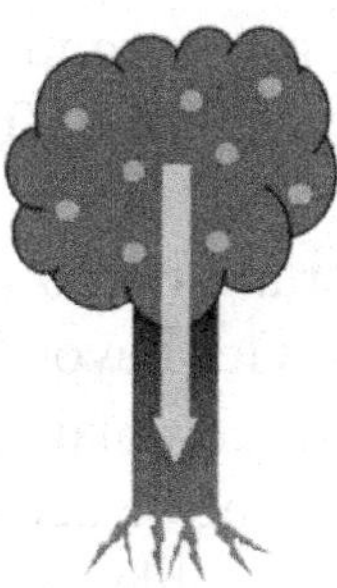

Symptoms / Behavior
What we overtly observe/hear

Patterns
What we hear and see over time

Desires / Motives
What is known by God

The fruit or symptoms are sometimes obvious. There are other times when you have to be quite observant to see or discern the heart issues. The trunk of the tree is patterns or themes you hear in their story or if you are part of their life, you see it over time. The roots of the tree represent the heart which is where all things originate (Proverbs 4:23, Luke 6:45). Don't settle for picking or rearranging fruit. Don't judge them for being stuck in a pattern of behavior that is sin (Galatians 6:1-2; & 1 Corinthians 6:11). Draw them out and help them see the heart issues driving their behavior.[1]

Most of us have been hurt by people assuming something about us without knowing us well, or presuming our motives based on very little information. A godly friend learns to ask heart-revealing questions and listen to understand, not just to respond. You move from fruit to root issues by discerning what is an obvious unwanted behavior (fruit), to how they think or predominate attitudes (trunk) to what they desire (root). An example of getting to the root is to ask what is going on in their life that is stressing them. Then, ask your friend what they want from that situation. What do they hope for as an outcome? It is important not to jump to conclusions (like Job's friends). Get beyond the rearranging of fruit—moving past complaints or venting—to getting to motives like comfort, security, pleasure, or control. Then you will be able to bring wise counsel that targets the heart.[2]

God deals with each individual instead of categorizing people. Because He loves us. In Galatians 5:19-23,

Paul is helping us determine who is saved and who is not saved. We are either rooted in the flesh, or rooted in the Spirit. Only you and Jesus know *for sure* if you are saved. You have to ask yourself the question as to whether or not you are saved as you examine the fruit you are bearing. We are not talking about one-time offenses, but rather a life marked by the fruit of the flesh that would be indicative of an unbeliever. *It is quite different to be struggling with a sin and fighting against it, and being comfortable with that sin while hiding it.*

There is a spiritual realm and enemies that are fighting against us to love God. If you are planted in the Spirit, the fruit of your life when threatened is not rivalry, division, anger, or jealousy. It is the opposite. The evidence of the Holy Spirit in your life is peace, goodness, faithfulness, gentleness, and self-control.

As believers, the way we fight should be extremely different than how the world fights. The enemy wants us to use his tactics and aim our arrows at one another. This keeps us distracted from the real battle–bringing darkness to light and sharing the Gospel with those who are searching and ready to accept Jesus. It means we are focused on kingdom work and we know who the real enemy is.

Grow in your understanding of who you are in Christ and who He is. Let these truths transcend your past, present, and future realities. *Then* you can create space for others to do the same. God's work supernaturally multiplies.

Parent Safety Resources (from Ch. 9):

I reached out to Eden's Glory, a local ministry that educates people about these dangers and provides a home where victims of trafficking can begin their healing journey. They shared the following tips with us to help parents be proactive in keeping their kids safe from today's threats:

Internet Safety:

- Smartphones and Social Media are highly addictive, creating dopamine levels that are similar to drugs, alcohol, and gambling
- All apps aren't either good or bad, they can be used for both
- Apps like TikTok, WhatsApp, Vaulty, SnapChat, Kik, Burn Note, Line, Whisper, Omegle, Ask, Blender, Tinder, YikYak, IMVU, Down, Badoo, Wickr, Photoswap, After School, Voxer, Tellonym, Tumbler, Yolo, Vault, Keepsafe, HIde it Pro, and Secret Calculator are all apps that have little to no parent controls, age requirements, little limitations on adult content, allow sexting, erases messages or have hidden messaging, are used for bullying, have GPS locators, allows chatting with random strangers, are used for "hooking-up" and rating how hot it was, allow explicit acts to be posted, request personal information, and more.

- Learn what emojis and the combination of emojis your child is sending through texts and other messaging apps mean.

Watch for:

- Change in behavior
- New belongings or expensive gifts
- Sleeping more during the day and at school
- Seem more on edge
- New and more passwords
- Increase in data usage
- Missing parts of messages
- Isolation
- No browser history

Response:

- Wait until 8th grade or longer for social media
- link your email or iCloud to their apps
- Use strict privacy settings
- Only allow computer use in community/public spaces
- Have open conversations about public posting and that nothing is "private"
- Set up parental controls on your child's phone
- Help them find a healthy mentor they can trust
- Turn off GPS locators
- Regularly review downloads
- Prevention and awareness: attend an internet safety class, invite Eden's Glory to speak to your church, community event, small group or school, keep up with new apps, continue to research

Additional notes from Chris and I on resources

Sacrifices we joyfully make so we can connect deeply with our kids include living on a single income so I can disciple, educate, nurture, and be present for our children full-time; monthly parent-child date nights that are inexpensive, intentional one-on-one connections; and, when they are between 10-12 years of age, taking them through *Passport to Purity* over a fun, two-day getaway–Chris with our son, and me with each of our girls–so we can talk about sex and God's beautiful intent for it. We also maintain genuine community with our brothers and sisters in Christ through weekend services and small group, so we have the support, love, and accountability we all need to be healthy individuals. We make time to spend with God regularly and help our kids know what it looks like to cultivate their relationship with Jesus.

We haven't perfected this, but the posture of our hearts is to invite Jesus in as we raise them to know their created purpose and worth. We are growing in how to lean into the fullness of His presence daily.

END NOTES

CHAPTER 1: WHAT IS IT

1. "Who In Your Congregation Suffers From Trauma," Care to Change https://caretochange.org/who-in-your-congregation-suffers-from-trauma/
2. "What Does God Say About PTSD?" Dr. Lucy Ann Moll, Biblical Counseling Center, https://biblicalcounselingcenter.org/what-does-god-say-about-ptsd/
3. "Trauma and the Significance of Meaning," Biblical Counseling Coalition www.biblicalcounselingcoalition.org/2017/08/09/trauma-and-the-significance-of-meaning/
4. "Biblical Counseling and Post Traumatic Stress Disorder (PTSD)," Reformed Biblical Coaching, https://reformedbiblicalcoaching.wordpress.com/2010/12/22/biblical-counseling-and-post-traumatic-stress-disorder-ptsd/
5. "Psychological Trauma: What Was Intended for Evil God Can Use for Good," Focus On The Family, www.focusonthefamily.com/parenting/psychological-trauma-what-was-intended-for-evil-god-can-use-for-good/

6. "Trauma In America, Chapter 1: Incidence of Trauma" Barna Reports https://barna.gloo.us/reports/trauma-in-america-chapter-1
7. "Sex Trafficking In America–2021 Report," Guardian Group https://guardiangroup.org/sex-trafficking-in-america-2021-report

CHAPTER 2: HOW DO I SORT THROUGH IT ALL

1. "Sex Trafficking In America–2021 Report," Guardian Group https://guardiangroup.org/sex-trafficking-in-america-2021-report

CHAPTER 3: MY SHEEP HEAR ME

1. "God, Self or Satan: What God's Voice Sounds Like," Roger Barrier, Preach It Teach It, https://preachitteachit.org/ask_roger/god-self-or-satan-what-gods-voice-sounds-like/
2. "Sex Trafficking In America–2021 Report," Guardian Group https://guardiangroup.org/sex-trafficking-in-america-2021-report

CHAPTER 4: WORTH YOUR TRUST

1. "Sex Trafficking In America–2021 Report," Guardian Group https://guardiangroup.org/sex-trafficking-in-america-2021-report

CHAPTER 5: HE DELIGHTS IN PROVING IT

1. "What Is Grace," John Piper, Desiring God https://www.desiringgod.org/interviews/what-is-grace
2. "The Theology of Uncomfortable Grace," Paul David Tripp, www.youtube.com/watch?v=2UXDyTo_iHM
3. "Punishment vs. Discipline," John Piper, www.desiringgod.org/interviews/is-pain-punishment-for-my-sin
4. "Best Of Series Dr. Paul Tripp on the Depth of God's Grace," CGN + Calvary Chapel, https://www.youtube.com/watch?v=5NFm7xk09RE
5. "Trafficking Terms," Shared Hope International, https://sharedhope.org/the-problem/trafficking-terms/

CHAPTER 6: IS IT A SIN TO FEAR

1. "The Art of Fixing What's Broken," (article and photos) Andrew Kessler, Medium, https://medium.com/article-group/the-art-of-fixing-whats-broken-9fd42c5f6893
2. "Trafficking Terms," Shared Hope International, https://sharedhope.org/the-problem/trafficking-terms/
3. "Sex Trafficking In America–2021 Report," Guardian Group https://guardiangroup.org/sex-trafficking-in-america-2021-report

CHAPTER 7: HOW THE PAST IS AFFECTING YOUR INTIMACY

1. "What's Trauma Denial?" Psych Central (blog), https://psychcentral.com/blog/denial-of-trauma-signs#whats-trauma-denial
2. "Meredith Andrews - Not For A Moment (After All) - Live," Meredith Andrews Music, https://www.youtube.com/watch?v=XD0cvWImVjA

CHAPTER 10: IS HE GRIEVING

1. "Rape Trauma Syndrome and its Affects on Christian Spirituality," Seattle Christian Counseling, https://seattlechristiancounseling.com/articles/rape-trauma-syndrome-effects-christian-spirituality

CHAPTER 11: IS HE GOOD

1. "When Suffering Enters Your Door," Paul David Tripp, https://www.youtube.com/watch?v=I25sdg9psK0
2. "Why Do Bad Things Happen To Good People?" Lee Strobel Explains, Hope On Demand, https://www.youtube.com/watch?v=BgKThCh0Jcc
3. "Why Did God Let It Happen?" Craig Roeschel, Life.Church, https://www.youtube.com/watch?v=N8nQYyLn6Nc

CHAPTER 12: WHO IS HE IN MY SUFFERING

1. "Don't Preach At Suffering People," Paul David Tripp, https://www.youtube.com/watch?v=IrfHNwU5ExU
2. "How Do I Find Hope in Suffering?" Paul David Tripp, The Gospel Coalition, https://www.youtube.com/watch?v=tOdFhQPgMpQ

CHAPTER 13: TIME WITH HIM

1. "Breaking Down the Connection Between Pornography and Sex Trafficking," Fight to End Exploitation, https://fighttoendexploitation.org/breaking-down-the-connection-between-pornography-and-sex-trafficking/

CHAPTER 14: WHERE IS HE LEADING YOU NOW

1. "Should I Find A Mentor?" Ask Paul Tripp, Paul David Tripp, https://www.youtube.com/watch?v=A3QInhj1hes

CHAPTER 15: GLORY TO GLORY

1. "Transformed From Glory To Glory - 2 Corinthians 3:18" Scriptural Grace, https://www.scripturalgrace.com/post/transformed-from-glory-to-glory-2-corinthians-3-18
2. "Research Reveals: The Root Cause of Sex Trafficking is Pornography," Friends of WPC Nepal, https://friendsofwpcnepal.org/overlooked-way-help-end-sex-trafficking/

CHAPTER 16: GLORY TO GLORY

1. Eden's Glory, www.edensglory.org

CHAPTER 17: HANDING OVER YOUR STORY FOR HIS PURPOSES

1. "What Causes the Sweet Smell of Rain in Arizona?" Ian Schwarts, Arizona's Family News 5, https://www.azfamily.com/2024/05/06/what-causes-sweet-smell-rain-arizona/
2. "Creosote Bush" photo, Earth Observatory, https://www.earthobservatory.nasa.gov/biome/seedcreosote.php

APPENDIX

1. "Listen by Walking," Garrett Higbee, Biblical Counseling Coalition, www.biblicalcounselingcoalition.org/2012/06/28/listening-by-walking/
2. "Helping a Friend in Need," Garrett Higbee, Biblical Counseling Coalition, www.biblicalcounselingcoalition.org/2021/09/01/helping-a-friend-in-need/

ABOUT THE AUTHOR

Crystal Persons is the founder of the Healing D.E.E.P.E.R. Community, a ministry designed for women ready to heal deeper than their brokenness. She and her husband, Chris, are parents of three beautiful children. After years of serving in local church ministry alongside her husband, Crystal has gained an insider's perspective on the hearts and lives of Christian women. Her mission is to cultivate transcendent community—where healing and redemption power usher in true freedom to all enslaved by their pasts.

HEALING D.E.E.P.E.R. WITH CRYSTAL PERSONS

DEVELOP AWARENESS

Are you battling against darkness? Or are you enslaved to it?

ESTABLISH A SAFE PLACE

Learning where and w/ whom you can walk out your healing journey.

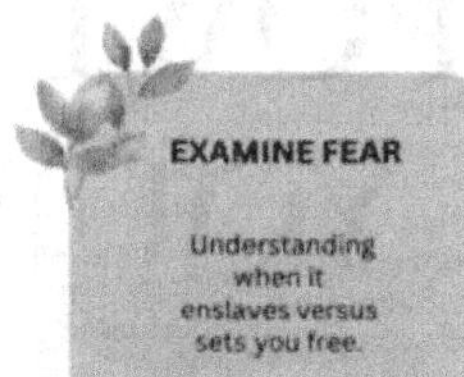

EXAMINE FEAR

Understanding when it enslaves versus sets you free.

PROCESS WHO GOD IS

Allowing who He is to transform your narrative.

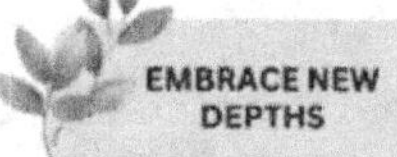

EMBRACE NEW DEPTHS

Growing your capacity as you heal, and increasing your stewardship.

REDEEM BROKENNESS

Embracing Kingdom purpose in your story.

SPEAKER

ONLINE COMMUNITY

COACH

IT'S TIME TO HEAL DEEPER THAN YOUR BROKENESS

CRYSTALPERSONS.COM

FIND HEALING AND ALLOW GOD'S REDEMPTIVE POWER TO REACH D.E.E.P.E.R. THAN YOUR BROKENNESS

FOLLOW ME ON INSTAGRAM

BIBLE STUDIES FREE RESOURCES